Love, For Short

Love, For Short

*Nine plays from works of
Anton Chekhov*

by
R. Andrew White
and James Serpento

from new translations by
R. Andrew White

with Jane Martsinovsky Hendricks

kingman
row

**KINGMAN ROW ENTERTAINMENT
JOHNSTON, IOWA**

TABLE OF CONTENTS

Anton Chekhov

The Bear

a joke in one movement

translated and adapted by
R. Andrew White

with Jane Martsinovsky Hendricks

This translation of *The Bear* was presented on a double bill with *The Proposal* by Act One Studios in Chicago, IL in March, 2004 and was directed by Zac Davis. The cast was as follows:

YELENA IVANOVNA POPOVA   Karen Yates

GRIGORY STEPANOVICH SMIRNOV   Mark Sharp

LUKA   Ken Peterson

This translation was also presented by Valparaiso University, Valparaiso, IN in February, 2000. It was directed by R. Andrew White. The costume design was by Ann Kessler, and the set design was by Alan Stalmah. The cast was as follows:

YELENA IVANOVNA POPOVA   Amber Hilgenkamp

GRIGORY STEPANOVICH SMIRNOV   Paul Oren

LUKA   Andrew Holmes

An early draft of the play was presented by Mad Genie Productions, Chicago, IL in March, 1994. It was directed by Christine Hartman, with the following cast:

YELENA IVANOVNA POPOVA   Tricia Kym Armstrong

GRIGORY STEPANOVICH SMIRNOV
                          David Mitchell Ghilardi

LUKA   R. Andrew White

CHARACTERS

YELÉNA IVÁNOVNA POPÓVA, a widowed estate owner with dimpled cheeks.

GRIGÓRY STEPÁNOVICH SMÍRNOV, a fairly young landowner.

LUKÁ, Popova's old servant.

This version of the text calls, at the end, for the appearance of a **GARDENER**, a **BLACKSMITH**, and a **WORKER**, all non-speaking roles, all wielding tools. It is also possible for the action at that moment to be performed simply by **LUKÁ** alone, carrying all of the tools (perhaps with difficulty).

SETTING

The action takes place in the living room of Popova's country estate

Anton Chekhov

The Bear

a joke in one movement

translated and adapted by
R. Andrew White

with Jane Martsinovksy Hendricks

(*YELENA IVANOVNA POPOVA is in deep mourning, fixing her gaze on a small photograph. LUKA stands nearby.*)

LUKA: Can we open a window at least? *(No response.)* You know. . . you know, this is not good. This is my conclusion. For what it's worth. Or for all you care. You're destroying yourself. The maid and the cook, they're out, picking berries, licking their fingers. The whole world's happy today. Not you, oh, no. *(Pause.)* Even the cat knows how to take pleasure in life. She's catching little birds out in the yard. *(Pause.)* Do you know what I tell people? "She's in training," I say. "She's in training to be a nun." A *nun.* *(Pause.)* It's been a year! You haven't left the house in a whole—

POPOVA: Why would I? I will never leave!

LUKA: (Here we go. . .)

POPOVA: My life is *ended.* He's in a grave—

LUKA: —and you've buried your*self* in these four walls, *he's* the dead one, what's *your* excuse?

POPOVA: *We both died.*

(Silence.)

LUKA: I won't listen to that! Nikoláy Mikháilovich died. That was God's will. We mourned for a while—and let it be. You cannot wear black and mourn for the next century. When my old lady kicked over. . .

POPOVA: (Oh, my God. . .)

LUKA: —*listen* now, all right, all. . .things aside for the moment, listen, I cried for a month, and that's it with her. *(Pause.)* She wasn't worth it. Not a whole century. *(Sighs.)* You've forgotten all of your neighbors. You won't visit them and won't let them set foot in here. We live, pardon the expression, like spiders—we never see the light of day. *(Pause.)* Mice ate holes in all my clothes. *(Pause.)* Town's full of nice people. There's a fine troop of soldiers over in Pavlov. *Officers.* Clean as candy. Can't look at 'em enough. And out in the camps, every Friday, there's a ball and—pay attention—an orchestra plays military music every day. . .You're young and beautiful. But, listen, beauty doesn't last forever. Ten years from now you'll want all those gentlemen and officers to look as you pass by and kick dust in their faces. But it'll be too late.

POPOVA *(decisively)***:** I ask you never to talk to me about it! You know from the moment Nikolái Mikháilovich died, life lost all meaning for me. You think I am alive, but that only *seems* to be. I promised myself, took a *vow* do you hear? To my *grave!* To never, ever take off this black dress. I loved that man. . .And, yes, I know it's no secret that, at times, he treated me unfairly. Yes, he could be cruel and. . .and even unfaithful, but *I* will be faithful to the grave and show him! I'll show him how I can love! He'll see from over there! From the *other* side, what kind of wife I was before he died.

LUKA: How about we take a nice walk? Maybe around the garden? Or, or a *ride*, eh? Oh yes. We can saddle up old Toby, and you can put a spur in his side.

POPOVA: Ah!

(POPOVA cries.)

LUKA: Mother of God, what is it with you?

POPOVA: He loved Toby. He always rode him to the Korchágins and the Vlásovs. Oh, how he could ride horses! How much grace there was in his form when he pulled the reins with all his might. Remember? Toby! Toby! Tell the servants to give him extra oats today.

LUKA: Yes, ma'am.

(The doorbell rings. . .long and loud.)

POPOVA *(startled)***:** Who's that? Tell them that I am not. . . *receiving* today.

LUKA: Of course, ma'am.

(LUKA exits. POPOVA looks at the photograph.)

POPOVA: You'll see, *Nicolas,*[1] how I can love. . . how I can forgive. My love will never die until I do, do you hear? Until my poor heart stops beating. *(Laughs through her tears.)* Aren't you ashamed? I'm a good girl, a faithful little wife, and have locked myself away, faithful to the grave. But you. . .aren't you ashamed of yourself, you chubby little child? You cheated on me, made scenes, left me alone for weeks on end. . .

(LUKA enters, worried.)

LUKA: Madam, there's, there's someone asking for you! He wants to see you. . .

POPOVA: Didn't you tell him that from the day of my husband's death I will see no one?

LUKA: Yes.

POPOVA: So?

---

[1] Addressing her husband with his name in French indicates Popova's sophistication.

LUKA: He doesn't want to listen. He said it was urgent (*I don't know. . .*)

POPOVA: I—will—see—no—one!

LUKA: I told him. . .but he's some kind of demon. . .he's cursing and forced his way inside. He's in the dining room now. So I. . .

POPOVA *(irritated)*: Alright, just send him in. What a boor!

(LUKA exits.)

POPOVA: How difficult these people are! What could he possibly need from me? Why must they destroy my. . . *(Sighs)* No, it's clear that I'll have to go into a convent. *(Thinking)* Yes, a convent. . .

(LUKA and SMIRNOV enter.)

SMIRNOV *(to LUKA)*: Idiot, you love to talk too much. . . Ass! *(Sees POPOVA; with dignity:)* Madam, may I have the honor to introduce myself: retired lieutenant of artillery and landowner Grigory Stepanovich Smirnov. I must disturb you about a matter of extreme urgency. Your late husband, with whom I had the *honor* of being acquainted, left me two note payables worth twelve hundred rubles.[2] So then *tomorrow* I have to make an interest payment to the bank. So I'm asking you, madam, to pay me my money today.

POPOVA: Twelve hundred.

SMIRNOV: Yes.

POPOVA: And why was my husband in debt to you?

SMIRNOV: He bought oats from me.

POPOVA *(sighing, to LUKA)*: Don't forget, Luka. Tell them to give Toby an extra bag of oats today!

(LUKA exits.)

---

[2] About $32,000 in present-day American currency.

POPOVA *(to SMIRNOV)*: If Nikolái Mikháilovich was in debt to you for twelve hundred rubles, I certainly will pay it; but you'll have to excuse me please, I don't have any cash on hand today.

SMIRNOV: Um...

POPOVA: But the day after tomorrow, my steward returns from the city, and of course I will have *him* pay you what you are owed. But today I cannot fulfill your wish. So I apologize. And you also should know that today is exactly seven months from the day my husband died. I am not inclined to be concerned with financial matters. I am in a mood.

SMIRNOV: Well, bankruptcy court doesn't do wonders for my disposition either. If I don't pay the interest tomorrow, I'll be turned inside-out. They'll seize my estate!

POPOVA: You'll have your money the day after tomorrow.

SMIRNOV: I don't need my money the day after tomorrow, I need it today.

POPOVA: I'm sorry, but I can't pay you today.

SMIRNOV: I can't wait until the day after tomorrow.

POPOVA: What can I do if I don't *have* it now?

SMIRNOV: So you can't pay me?

POPOVA: I can't.

SMIRNOV: So that's it?

POPOVA: I guess so.

SMIRNOV: Your last word? You're sure?

POPOVA: I'm sure.

SMIRNOV: Thank you very much, and I'll remember this. *(Starts to leave, and then...)* You know, it's funny, I ran into an old friend of mine the other day—the tax collector.

SMIRNOV *(cont'd)*: And he said "My goodness, Grigory Stepanovich, why are you always angry?" Well, excuse me, why shouldn't I be angry? I'm desperate for money. Since yesterday morning I've been driving around to everyone who owes me money, and not one of them could pay me. I'm tired as a dog, spent the night in some godforsaken tavern next to the vodka keg. And now here I am, forty miles from home, thinking I'll get what's owed me, and instead I get "I'm in a mood" and everyone wonders why I'm so angry!

POPOVA: Exactly what part of what I said are you not clear on? I told you: *The day after tomorrow* my steward returns and *then* you will get your money.

SMIRNOV: And I haven't come to see your steward. I came to see you. Why in the hell, pardon my language, would I want to see your steward?

POPOVA: Kind sir. My. . .*ears* are not accustomed to these . . . *colorful* expressions you seem to be so fond of using. Nor am I accustomed to the tone of your voice. And I am not going to listen to you any longer.

(She leaves quickly.)

SMIRNOV: Oh please. "I am in a mood," she says. And he died *seven months ago?* But what about me? Do I or don't I have to pay the interest on my mortgage or not? I ask you. Do I or don't I? Well, your husband is dead, you're "in a mood," but you have some trick up your sleeve. . .Your steward is gone, so to hell with him. What am I supposed to do? Fly away from the bill collectors in a hot air balloon? No, I have a better idea. Why don't I just bash my head into a brick wall? I go to see Grúzdev—"Oh I'm sorry. He's not here." Yaroshévich ran away and hid. And then there was Kurítzin. . .He's lucky I didn't throw him through that window. Mazútov has a stomach ache. Cholera. *(Beat.)* And this one's "in a mood." *(Beat.)* No money. I was too nice to them all, you see? So they take *advantage*, they turn me into some kind of clown. I'm their little rag doll, their little plaything. *(Very calm.)* All right. That's good.

SMIRNOV *(cont'd)*: They will get to know me then. For I will sit right here until she pays. *(Sits. Muses.)* Let's see. . .how angry am I today? *(Checks his wrists.)* Oh. My veins are just about to pop. Mm-hmm. *(Takes a little breath.)* And I can barely breathe. I am a fool. That is what I am. *(Screams.)* Servant!

(LUKA enters.)

LUKA: What do you want?

SMIRNOV: Kvass! Water! I don't care!

(LUKA exits.)

SMIRNOV *(to audience)*: So. *I'm* about to hang myself. *She's* "in a mood." *I'm* trying to decide between a rope or a gun. *She* is "not inclined to be concerned with money things." *(Pause.)* And there you have female logic. And that's why I don't like women. That's why I'd rather smoke a cigar on a barrel of gunpowder than talk to a woman.

(LUKA enters.)

LUKA *(giving water to SMIRNOV)*: Water. Madame is sick and not receiving.

SMIRNOV: Get out!

(LUKA leaves.)

SMIRNOV: "Sick and not receiving." I will sit here until I have my money. Be sick for a week. Fine. I'll be here a week. Be sick for a year. Fine. A year it is. *(Pause.)* I will have what's mine. *(Pause.)* You won't get me with that long black dress and those. . .sweet little dimples. *(Pause.)* I know about dimples. *(Yells out the window.)* Semyón! Unsaddle! We're not leaving anytime soon! I'm staying! Tell them at the stables to give the horses some oats! You idiot! You did it again! The left trace horse is tangled up in the reins! *(Walks away from the window.)* Damn, I feel sick. . .It's unbearably hot in here. No one will pay me, couldn't sleep all last night, and the one wearing black is "in a mood." Gives me a headache. *(Beat.)* Vodka would help. I'll have a drink. *(Screams.)* Servant!

(LUKA enters.)

LUKA: What do you want?

SMIRNOV: A glass of vodka!

(LUKA goes out.)

SMIRNOV: Oof! *(Sits down and looks himself over.)* Look at me. What a sight. Covered in forty miles of dust, dirty boots, haven't bathed, haven't brushed my hair, jacket's covered in straw. I must've looked like a thief to the lady. *(Yawns.)* It was probably rude for me to show up in her living room looking the way I do. Well, excuse me, I'm not a visitor but a creditor, and the creditors don't dress for a garden party when they bang on *my* door.

(LUKA enters and gives SMIRNOV a glass of vodka.)

LUKA: You look agitated, sir—

SMIRNOV *(angrily)*: What?

LUKA: Nothing, I. . .nothing. . .I was only. . .

SMIRNOV: What are you babbling about?! Be quiet!

LUKA *(aside)*: He just barges in, the devil. . .brings us nothing but trouble.

(LUKA exits.)

SMIRNOV: Ah! How angry I am! So angry I could pulverize the whole world. . . *(Yells.)* Servant!

(POPOVA enters, eyes downcast.)

POPOVA: Kind sir, in my time of solitude, I long ago grew unaccustomed to the sound of the human voice. So you can imagine how I cannot tolerate your yelling. Go away and leave me in peace.

SMIRNOV: Pay me my money, and I will leave.

POPOVA: I said to you in plain Russian that I don't have the money now. You'll have to wait until the day after tomorrow.

SMIRNOV: And I said to you in plain Russian that I don't need the money the day after tomorrow. I need it now. If I don't pay them, they'll hang me!

POPOVA: What can I do if I don't have the money?

SMIRNOV: So you won't pay me?

POPOVA: I *can't* pay you!

SMIRNOV: Then I am going to sit. *(He sits.)* On this chair. You'll pay me the day after tomorrow? Wonderful! I will wait. I will sit here until then. ON THIS CHAIR. Right here I will sit. *(Jumps up.)* Alright, give me the money. I have to have it. I have to pay interest. Do you think I'm joking?

POPOVA: Kind gentleman, I ask you not to scream. This isn't a stable.

SMIRNOV: I'm not asking you about stables, but about the fact that I have to pay interest on my mortgage tomorrow!

POPOVA: You don't know how to control yourself in the presence of a woman.

SMIRNOV: No. I can control myself in the presence of a woman!

POPOVA: No you can't. You are unrefined and rude. *Proper* people don't talk like that to a woman.

SMIRNOV: What, do you want me to speak in French? *Madame, je vous en prie. . .*

POPOVA: . . .no no no. . .

SMIRNOV: . . .how pleased I'd be if you would condescend to pay me my money. Ah! *Pardon.* . .So sorry to have bothered you. What lovely weather, and that black dress suits you so well!

(He bows.)

POPOVA: You're not funny, only rude.

SMIRNOV *(mimicking)***:** "Not funny, only rude." *(Pause.)*

SMIRNOV *(cont'd)*: Look, in my time, I've seen more women than you've seen sparrows. I fought *duels* over three women, ran away from twelve and *nine* ran away from *me*. *(Pause.)* So you see, I was a fool once.

POPOVA: Once?

SMIRNOV *(pause)*: I spoke words as sweet as honey. My heart'd break like a string of pearls. I polished my shoes. . . loved, suffered, sighed at the moon, came unglued over love, melted, fasted. . .I loved passionately, madly. . .devil take me. Oh I know love. Believe me. I was a little puppy. I'd wag my tail about women's rights and so on. Story of my life. But not now. I'm no one's servant. Enough of that! Black, passionate eyes and soft lips and sweet dimples. I've had my fill of that. No more whispers in the moonlight for this man. No more caresses in the night and. . .and gentle sighs—I wouldn't give anything for it. *(Beat.)* All women, present company excluded, are *web*-weaving, *false* of heart, *talk*-behind-your-back *liars*. *(Beat.)* And what concerns this here thing. . . *(Taps forehead)* . . .well, excuse my honesty, but you'll find more *intelligentsia* building nests out in the trees than you will in skirts.

POPOVA: Oh now that's—

SMIRNOV: No, now think about this. Think. You look at a woman, what do you see? A *poetic composition*, an ethereal *goddess* all bedecked in muslin. That's a million joys, I agree. *But. (Leans in on the back of a chair.)* Look into her *soul*. Now what do you see? A *crocodile! (The chair cracks and breaks.)* But the thing that upsets me the most: this, this crocodile for some reason. . .*contends*. . . that its role, no no, its *privilege* is what? *Tender feelings!* That's crazy! Go ahead and hang me on a nail by my feet if a woman can love anything except her lapdog! A woman in love whines and cries. And the man—what's he do?—he suffers and sacrifices while she rustles her skirt and leads him by the nose. You have the misfortune of being a woman. So you must know what I'm talking about. You know the nature of women. Now just be honest with me. Have you ever, *ever* in your lifetime seen a woman who was honest?

SMIRNOV *(cont'd)*: Who was true? *(No answer.)* See? You haven't. Except for the old ugly ones.

POPOVA: Oh!

SMIRNOV: The day you'll see an honest woman is the day cats grow horns!

POPOVA *(pause)*: So, in all of your wisdom. . .

SMIRNOV: . . .yes. . .

POPOVA: . . .your carefully-considered opinion. . .

SMIRNOV: . . .that's right. . .

POPOVA: . . .as I see you are a Learned Creature. . .please tell me who do *you* think is honest and true?

SMIRNOV: Men.

(POPOVA laughs hysterically.)

SMIRNOV: What—

(He can't get a word in, she's laughing so hard now.)

POPOVA: Men!

(She's starting to gain control of her laughter.)

POPOVA: Well that means a lot coming from you. I'll tell you about men. I know and did know just about the best of them. And that was *my* man. I loved my husband with all of my soul, and I gave him my youth, my joy and my life. I worshiped him do you hear? And this "best of men," this *paragon* lied to me. After he died, one day I was cleaning up some of his things, and I opened up a desk drawer and found some letters. Actually a lot of letters. . .from other women. It all suddenly became clear to me why he would leave me for weeks at a time. But now I don't know why it was such a surprise, because he cheated on me in front of my face. *(Pause.)* Yes, I'll tell you about men. He wasted my money and made a big joke out of my feelings. And I loved him. And now he lies dead in the ground, and I'm *still* true to him. Buried in four walls.

POPOVA *(cont'd)*: And so help me God, I'll wear this black dress until I die.

SMIRNOV *(pause)*: You're so. . .*deep*. Who're you trying to fool? No, I'm sure to some eighteen-year-old half-baked poet, *with a beret*, who might wander by the house, you look like a work of art. "My God that's where she lives. The mysterious woman who, because of her love for her husband, has buried herself within four walls." But you don't fool me. You're not a work of art. You are, however, a piece of work.

POPOVA: *What?*

SMIRNOV: You buried yourself alive, but you didn't forget to powder your nose.

POPOVA: Don't you *dare* talk to me like that!

SMIRNOV: Don't yell at me. I'm not your servant!

POPOVA: I'm not yelling! *You're* yelling!

SMIRNOV: Well excuse me! I'm not a woman! I express my thoughts *directly*!

POPOVA: Get out now!

SMIRNOV: Pay me my money—

POPOVA: I won't give you a *kopek*!

SMIRNOV: Look, I'm not your husband, so you can save your little scene.

(SMIRNOV sits.)

POPOVA: You sat down!

SMIRNOV: Yes I did.

POPOVA: I told you to leave!

SMIRNOV: You know what I want.

POPOVA: I'm not going to talk to you! Go!

(They look at each other. A long pause.)

POPOVA: Fine.

(She rings the bell and LUKA enters.)

POPOVA: Luka, show this gentleman to the door.

LUKA *(approaches SMIRNOV)*: All right, you've been asked to leave.

SMIRNOV *(leaps out of the chair)*: Quiet! I'll toss you like a salad!

LUKA *(grabs his chest)*: My heart!

(LUKA falls into an armchair and catches his breath.)

POPOVA: Where's Dásha? *(Yells.)* Dásha! Pelegáya! Dásha!

(Rings bell wildly.)

LUKA: They're all picking berries. I need some water.

POPOVA *(to SMIRNOV)*: Get the hell out of here!

SMIRNOV: You're being so rude.

POPOVA *(clenches her fists and stomps her feet)*: You filthy peasant! *(Growls.)* You're a monster! You're a bear!

SMIRNOV: How was that? What did you say?

POPOVA: I said that you are a bear! Bear bear BEAR!

SMIRNOV: Are you insulting me?

POPOVA: A *genius* walks among us!

SMIRNOV: You think you can just stand there and *insult* me?

POPOVA: Think? I *know* I can!

SMIRNOV: I see. It's your *birth*right, is that how it is? Because you're a woman? *(Pause.)* I challenge you to a duel.

LUKA: Oh God. Water.

SMIRNOV: To a *duel!*

POPOVA: Because you have big fists and a throat like an ox, you think I'm afraid of you? You think I'm afraid of filth like you?

SMIRNOV: Pistols! I don't care that, that you're a woman. A simple, weak, sniveling woman!

POPOVA *(trying to scream over him)***:** BEAR! BEAR! BEAR!

SMIRNOV: Women think that only men should pay for insults. To hell with that! What's fair is fair said the smelly old Bear!

POPOVA: You want a duel? You want a duel?

SMIRNOV: This minute!

POPOVA: I'll give you a duel! I'll go get my husband's pistols. Don't you move.

(Runs out the door. Sticks her head back in.)

POPOVA: I'll stick a bullet in your bear head!

(She goes.)

SMIRNOV *(shouts after her)***:** I'll shoot you like a baby chicken! *(To himself.)* I'm not a little boy.

LUKA *(gets to his knees, speaking rapidly)***:** Dear Father in Heaven have mercy on me pity me I'm an old man. . .

SMIRNOV *(not listening to him)***:** There's your *equal rights*. Now you've gone too far, eh? Now it's my *duty* to kill you. "I'll stick a bullet in your bear head," she says with those. . . supple lips, those flashing eyes. This is a *real* woman. That's the first time I've ever heard a true word come out of a woman's mouth.

(LUKA quietly mutters a prayer.)

SMIRNOV: This woman, this is a woman I understand. She's more than makeup and powder. This one's smoke and fire. *(Pause.)* It'd be a shame to kill this one!

LUKA *(still in prayer)***:** (Make him leave.)

SMIRNOV: I like her. Yes, I like those dimples. I may even *forgive* her.

(POPOVA enters with two guns.)

POPOVA *(holds up the guns)*: Look at these.

SMIRNOV: Beautiful.

(She walks closer to him and aims one at him.)

POPOVA: How do I shoot?

SMIRNOV: What?

POPOVA: You'll have to show me how to shoot. I've never held a gun.

SMIRNOV: Well. . .

LUKA *(finishing his prayer)*: Save us dear Lord and keep us in your grace. Amen. *(Gets up. Sheepishly.)* I'll go and find the gardener and the blacksmith. . . *(Leaving.)* Why do these things happen to us?

(LUKA is gone.)

SMIRNOV: There are several kinds of pistols. There are special dueling pistols. That would be the *Mortimer*, which is a percussion-lock pistol. But these you have here are Smith and Wesson *revolvers*. Triple action, ejector and central fire. Beautiful guns. Cost at least ninety rubles for the pair. *(Stands close to her and helps her aim.)* You uh, have to hold the revolver like this.

POPOVA: Like this?

SMIRNOV: Yes. Then you raise the sight like so. Aim. Head a little back. Stretch out your arm more. No no, here, it should be like this. *(Adjusts her arm.)* Like so. Then with this finger squeeze this little thing.

POPOVA: It's a trigger, I know *that*.

SMIRNOV *(beat)*: And that's it. Only the most important rule: don't get excited. Aim slowly. . .Aim so that your arm doesn't shake.

POPOVA: Good. I'm not comfortable shooting in the house. Let's go outside.

SMIRNOV: Let's go.

(They start to leave. SMIRNOV stops.)

SMIRNOV: But I'm warning you. . .I'll shoot into the air.

POPOVA: Whatever for?

SMIRNOV: Because. . .um. *Because.*

POPOVA: Are you *scared?*

SMIRNOV: No, it's just. . .that's my business.

POPOVA: Well, don't fool around with me. I won't be satisfied until I've put a bullet in your head. . . that head that I hate so much. Come on. Are you a coward?

SMIRNOV: Yes, I'm. . .a coward.

POPOVA: Don't lie to me. Why don't you want to fight?

SMIRNOV: Because I. . .I *like* you.

POPOVA *(laughs)***:** You like me? Please! *(She points to the door.)* Come on!

(SMIRNOV puts down the gun, picks up his hat and starts to go. Just before he reaches the door, he stops and turns around and looks at POPOVA. The two stare at each other for a moment. SMIRNOV walks close to her.)

SMIRNOV: Listen, are you still angry? I know I acted a little crazy, but please understand. . .how can I say this? The thing is, well, you see, honestly, nothing like this has ever happened to me. *(Yells.)* Can I help it that I like you? *(Clutches the back of a chair; it breaks.)* Such fragile furniture you have. I like you! Do you understand that? I think I *love* you!

POPOVA: Oh my God.

SMIRNOV: Listen—

POPOVA: No, I hate you!

SMIRNOV: God, what a woman! Never in my life have I seen anything like it! I'm caught! I'm dead! I'm a mouse in a trap!

(POPOVA points the gun at him. She keeps it aimed at him all through his next line.)

POPOVA: Get out of here.

SMIRNOV: Go ahead. Pull the trigger. I'd give anything to die under the gaze of those wonderful dark eyes! To die from the revolver held in that tiny velvet hand! I'm insane. Make up your mind now, because if I leave here, then we will never see each other again. Decide. *(No answer.)* Oh, I'm a fine man. I'm a landowner, a respectable man, I make ten thousand a year. I have wonderful horses. *(Beat.)* Would you like to be my wife?

POPOVA: Go away or I'll shoot.

SMIRNOV: I know I know! I've lost my mind! I don't understand anything!

POPOVA: Then get your gun!

SMIRNOV: I've gone mad! I fell in love! Like a boy, like a *boy*!

(SMIRNOV grabs POPOVA by the hand. She shrieks in pain.)

SMIRNOV: I love you. *(Gets on his knees.)* I love you like I've never loved before. Twelve women I left. Nine left me. But not one of them, not *one* I ever loved like, like you. I've melted. I'm here on my knees, like a fool offering you my hand. I haven't loved for five years. I promised myself, took a *vow* do you hear? To my *grave!* That I would never fall in love again. And here I am. Here I. . .am. *(Pause.)* So what is it? Yes or No?

(POPOVA is silent. SMIRNOV gets up and starts to leave.)

POPOVA: Stand still.

(SMIRNOV stops.)

POPOVA: No. Leave. No. Stay. No. Leave, *leave!* I hate you! No I don't. Yes I do. *(Growls.)* Oh you have no idea how mad I am. *(She throws down the revolver.)* Damn thing made my fingers numb. What are you waiting for? Get out.

SMIRNOV: Forgive me.

POPOVA: Go!

(He starts to leave.)

POPOVA: Where are you going? Stay! No, go!

(SMIRNOV walks toward her.)

POPOVA: No, don't come near me. I'm mad at you.

SMIRNOV: I'm mad at myself. Fell in love like a schoolboy. Went down on my knees. I love you, *need* you, don't you see? *(Puts his arms around her waist.)* I'll never forgive myself.

POPOVA: Get away from me! Take your hands off me! I hate you. I hate you. Let's go fight.

(A long kiss. LUKA runs in with the GARDENER, BLACKSMITH and a WORKER, all wielding farm tools. They see the couple kissing and stop at the door.)

POPOVA: Luka! Tell them not to give Toby any oats today.

CURTAIN

Anton Chekhov

The Proposal

a joke in one movement

translated and adapted by
R. Andrew White

This translation of *The Proposal* was presented by Valparaiso University, Valparaiso, IN in February, 2000. It was directed by R. Andrew White. The costume design was by Ann Kessler, and the set design was by Alan Stalmah. The cast was as follows:

STEPAN STEPANOVICH CHUBUKOV   David Kelch

NATALYA STEPANOVNA   Deborah Craft

IVAN VASILYEVICH LOMOV   Justin Bayle

CHARACTERS

STEPÁN STEPÁNOVICH CHUBUKÓV, landowner.

NATÁLYA STEPÁNOVNA, his daughter, 25 years old.

IVÁN VASÍLYEVICH LÓMOV, their neighbor, a landowner and hypochondriac.

SETTING

Chubukov's living room on his country estate.

Anton Chekhov

The Proposal

a joke in one movement

translated and adapted by R. Andrew White

(CHUBUKOV in the living room of his country estate. IVAN VASILYEVICH LOMOV enters, wearing tails and white gloves.)

CHUBUKOV *(goes to him)***:** Why of all the people! My dear old friend! Such a pleasure, such a surprise! *(Shakes his hand.)* Holy Moses! How have you been?

LOMOV: Oh. . .Thank you. How've you been doing?

CHUBUKOV: Oh we just keep plowing right along, with the help of your kind prayers, and so on. . .Please, please sit down. You know. . . you know, it's a bad thing for a man to forget his neighbors. *(Noticing LOMOV 's clothes.)* But why so formal? On your way to someplace important?

LOMOV: No, I've come to see you.

CHUBUKOV: But in tails? Gloves? What, is it New Year's Eve?

LOMOV: Well. You see, the thing is. . .you see. . .my dear . . . *(Seizes CHUBUKOV by the arm.)* My dear Stepan Stepánich. I've called on you today for a. . .a favor, a blessing really. If it's not too much trouble, that is. In the past, you might remember, I have had the, the honor of asking for your help more than once.

LOMOV *(cont'd)***:** And you have always been so, so. . .how can I put it. . .so generous in your. . .I'm sorry. Nerves got the best of me. . .so then, today, dear Stepan Stepánich, I've come to ask you for for. . .for. . .a glass of water.

CHUBUKOV *(leads LOMOV to a pitcher of water where he drinks; to audience)***:** He wants money. He's not getting any. *(Back to LOMOV.)* So what do you need?

LOMOV: You see my. . .my esteemed Stepanovich. . .I mean Stepan Esteemovich. . .I mean. . .what I want to say is. . .I feel, I feel, that you are the only person who can help me and I know of course that I in no way shape or form deserve. . .I mean I've done nothing that would ever give me the right to—

CHUBUKOV: Spit it out before it kills you, boy!

LOMOV: Yes. All right then. Here we go. The point, the point. . . The thing is. . .I have come to ask for your daughter's hand in marriage.

CHUBUKOV *(pause)***:** Come again?

LOMOV: I have the honor to ask. . .

CHUBUKOV *(interrupting)***:** Mother of God! Ivan Vasilyevich! My dear, dear, dear boy! Of course, of course! With honor! *(He hugs LOMOV.)* Oh, I've wished. *(Kisses him.)* I've prayed! All of these many years! *(Tears are coming.)* Do you know, do you know my boy that I have always loved you as a son? As my *blood!* And may God above grant you both love, joy and so on. . .I'm standing here like a fool. I'm dumbstruck with joy! Right down to my soul! *(Starts to go out.)* I'll go find Natasha. . .

LOMOV *(touched)***:** Stepan Stepánich! *(CHUBUKOV stops.)* Do you think she will. . .I mean, may I count on her. . . consent?

CHUBUKOV: Ohhhh! And you such a fine young man? Look at you. How could she refuse? Why I'm sure she's in love with you, crazy as a kitten and so on. . .Now you stay right here.

(CHUBUKOV goes out.)

LOMOV *(alone):* So cold. I'm shaking all over, like I'm about to take an exam. But the main thing: Make up your mind and do it. Because if you wait, if you're all talk. . .it'll never happen. You're standing around. You're stalling, waiting on "the woman of your dreams." If you wait on true love, you'll never get married. *(He shivers.)* Now. Natalya Stepanovna. There's a fine woman. Good housekeeper, educated too. Not bad-looking. What more do I need? But I'm so nervous. . .my ears are even ringing. *(Drinks more water.)* I have to get married! I can't stay single! First, I'm thirty-five: "the critical age." Second, I must have a quiet, normal life. I have a heart condition. I keep having palpitations. And on top of it, I flare up so quickly! And now my lip's trembling and my eyelid's twitching. . .But the worst comes when I go to bed. I lay there, I just start to doze off and. . .*Stab!* Something pulls in my left side. *Bang!* It shoots right up my shoulder and into my head! I leap out of bed like a madman. And I walk, and I walk. . .and then I slowly lay down again. Calm, calm. I start to doze and. . .*Stab!* It's back! In my side! Up to my head! If it happens once, it happens twenty times!

(NATALYA STEPANOVNA enters.)

NATALYA STEPANOVNA: Well, by golly, it's you. Papa said there was a merchant here. Said he "come for the goods." Hello, Ivan Vasilyevich!

LOMOV: Hello, my dear Natalya Stepanovna!

NATALYA STEPANOVNA: Oh look. And me in my nighty! What a mess! Shucking peas, you know. Have to dry 'em. Now why haven't you been over for a visit in so long? Have a seat.

(They sit.)

NATALYA STEPANOVNA: You've been keeping from us! You want some lunch?

LOMOV: No thank you, I already ate.

NATALYA STEPANOVNA: Then have a smoke. Look, here are some matches. Wonderful weather, eh? Wonderful.

NATALYA STEPANOVNA *(cont'd)*: Rained torrents yesterday, though, the farm hands couldn't get a lick of work done all day. How many stacks did you bail? I had the whole meadow cut, if you want to know. I was so set on getting it done. S'pose I'll pay though. 'Fraid the hay's gonna rot. Might've done better to wait after all. . .ah well. . .But look at you! What's all this? Don't think I've seen you dressed so fine, tails and all! What're you up to, a *Ball?* Is that it? You look very handsome, I must say, but why are you all dressed up?

LOMOV: My dear Natalya Stepanovna. . .The thing is, I have come to ask you to. . .to. . .to listen to what I have to say. This might take you unawares, might even. . .ruffle your *feathers*, so to speak. . .but the thing is. . . *(To audience.)* So horribly cold!

NATALYA STEPANOVNA: What's the matter? *(Pause.)* Well?

LOMOV: I'll try to make this short. My dear Natalya Stepanovna, as you know, I have had the, the honor of knowing your family for a long time, ever since I was a little boy. My late aunt and her husband from whom I, as I believe you know, inherited my estate, always treated your father and your late mother with deep respect. The Lomovs and the Chubukovs have always had a very friendly. . .you might even say *familial* relationship. And then there's our land. The borders of our soil are so close together. If you remember, my Little Ox Meadows touch your birches.

NATALYA STEPANOVNA: I'm sorry. I need to interrupt here. You just said "*My* Little Ox Meadows." They aren't yours.

LOMOV: No, they're mine.

NATALYA STEPANOVNA: Oh, really? The Little Ox Meadows are ours, not yours.

LOMOV: No, my dear Natalya Stepanovna. I believe they're mine.

NATALYA STEPANOVNA: Well that's news to me. And how'd they come to be yours?

LOMOV: How? *(Pause.)* I'm talking about the Little Ox Meadows. The ones that form the wedge between your birches and Burnt Marsh.

NATALYA STEPANOVNA: Exactly. They're ours.

LOMOV: No, my dear Natalya Stepanovna, you're mistaken, they're mine.

NATALYA STEPANOVNA: I see, and how long have they been yours?

LOMOV: For as long as I can remember. They've always belonged to the Lomovs.

NATALYA STEPANOVNA: Well that doesn't make sense, Ivan Vasilyevich.

LOMOV: No, no, no. My dear Natalya Stepanovna, it's all there in the documents. Now, there was a dispute over the ownership at one time, it's true, but now that's all been settled. Everyone knows they're mine. There's no argument about that. You see, my aunt's grandmother loaned the Little Ox Meadows, rent-free, for an indefinite period to your father's grandfather's peasants as compensation for their making bricks for her. Now, your father's grandfather's peasants used the Meadows rent-free for some forty-odd years and came to think of them as their own. But, you see, when the serfs were emancipated[3]. . .

NATALYA STEPANOVNA: No no no no no! Not true! Here's how it is: My Papa and great grandpapa have always claimed that land because they knew, you see, that their property extended *up to* Burnt Marsh—so that would make the Little Ox Meadows ours, wouldn't it? What's there to argue? I don't understand. This is ridiculous.

LOMOV: I'll show you the papers.

---

[3] Lomov refers to Alexander II's Emancipation Reform of 1861, which abolished serfdom and afforded serfs the equal rights of free citizens.

NATALYA STEPANOVNA: What is this? A joke, or are you making fun of me? It's astonishing. We own a piece of land for almost three hundred years, and then one day you walk in and tell us it's not ours! Am I *hearing* this? Ivan Vasilyevich, I mean, it's not that the Meadows amount to much. A dozen acres or so. . .wouldn't bring more than three hundred rubles. It's the injustice of it that infuriates me. Say whatever you want, but I won't tolerate injustice.

LOMOV: Listen to me, please! Your father's grandfather's peasants, as I have already had the honor to explain to you, made bricks for my aunt's grandmother. My aunt's grandmother, wanting to reward them with a favor. . .

NATALYA STEPANOVNA *(interrupting)***:** Grandfather, grandmother, aunt. . .I don't understand any of this! The Little Ox Meadows are ours and that's that.

LOMOV: They're mine!

NATALYA STEPANOVNA: Ours! Go ahead and stand there makin' a fuss for two days, put on fifteen dressy jackets, but the Meadows are still ours, ours, ours! *(Pause.)* Look. I don't want to take what's yours, and I won't give up what's mine, thank you very much.

LOMOV: I don't even *want* the Meadows. It's just the principle of the thing. . .Look, if you want them, I'll give them to you.

NATALYA STEPANOVNA: Well, I might just give them to you since they're already ours! This has me confused, Ivan Vasilyevich. Up to this time, up to this moment, we always thought of you as a good neighbor, as a friend. Didn't we last year lend you our thresher? Had to put off our own threshing clear 'til November. And here you walk in and treat us like a bunch of gypsies! Giving me my own land. You're no neighbor. Truth be told, you're downright cruel, if you want to know!

LOMOV: Oh, I see, I see. So you're calling me some kind of squatter, is that it? Well, Madam, I have never in my life taken another man's land.

LOMOV *(cont'd):* So don't go pointing fingers at me! *(Quickly goes for more water.)* The Little Ox Meadows are mine!

NATALYA STEPANOVNA: Liar, ours!

LOMOV: Mine!

NATALYA STEPANOVNA: Liar, ours! I'll prove it to you! I'll send my mowers down there today!

LOMOV: What?

NATALYA STEPANOVNA: My men. Mowing them. Today!

LOMOV: I'll throw 'em out on their necks!

NATALYA STEPANOVNA: You wouldn't dare!

LOMOV *(clutching his heart):* The Little Ox Meadows are mine! Do you understand? Mine!

NATALYA STEPANOVNA: You shut it! You can scream 'til you're hoarse at home, but don't you dare raise your voice in my house!

LOMOV: Madam, if I weren't suffering from these terrible, painful palpitations, if the veins weren't throbbing in my temples, my tone with you would be very different right now! *(Shouts.)* The Little Ox Meadows are mine!

NATALYA STEPANOVNA: Ours!

LOMOV: Mine!

NATALYA STEPANOVNA: *Ours!*

LOMOV: *Mine!*

(CHUBUKOV rushes in.)

CHUBUKOV: What in the name of. . .What's the matter—?

NATALYA STEPANOVNA: Papa!

CHUBUKOV: —all the shouting. . .

NATALYA STEPANOVNA: Papa, tell this gentleman who the Little Ox Meadows belong to!

CHUBUKOV (to *LOMOV*): My little hen, they're ours.

LOMOV: But please, Stepan Stepanich, be reasonable. How can that be when you know that my aunt's grandmother gave the Meadows free of charge for temporary use to your grandfather's peasants. The peasants used the land for some forty years and came to think of it as their own. . .

CHUBUKOV: Whoa! Excuse me. . .

LOMOV: . . .but after the emancipation. . .

CHUBUKOV: . . .*excuse* me! My son, you're forgetting: those peasants never paid your grandmother a thing because they were already thrashing out who owned the Meadows and so on. . .But now it's all been settled. Everyone knows, even every *dog* in town knows it's mine. You haven't seen the documents?

LOMOV: I'll prove it's mine!

CHUBUKOV: You can't, my dear boy.

LOMOV: I can and I will!

CHUBUKOV: Mother of God, why are you yelling? I don't want what's yours and I'm not giving up what's mine. And besides, if you keep acting like a lunatic, I'd give the Meadows to the peasants over you anyway!

LOMOV: You don't have the right to—

CHUBUKOV: I know my *rights*. Now don't bull up against me, son. I'm old enough to be your father, so just calm yourself down.

LOMOV: You call my land yours, and then tell me "to calm myself down"? Ha! That's rich!

CHUBUKOV: Good neighbors do not behave this way.

LOMOV: Fine proverb coming from a squatter!

CHUBUKOV: What? What's that?

NATALYA STEPANOVNA: Papa, send the mowers down there now!

CHUBUKOV: Sir, did you say what I think you said?

NATALYA STEPANOVNA: The Little Ox Meadows belong to us, and I will never give them up.

LOMOV: We'll see! I'll take you to court! That'll show you!

CHUBUKOV: Go ahead. You go out and find the highest court you can! I know you. You sit around and just wait for a chance to drag some innocent man to court! You petty little shriveled up liar! You Lomovs were always liars! Every last one of you!

LOMOV: You keep my family out of this. We Lomovs have always been a family of honor! Not one of us was ever hauled into court over embezzlement like your grandfather!

CHUBUKOV: And not one of us was ever insane like everyone in your family!

NATALYA STEPANOVNA: Every last one of 'em!

CHUBUKOV: And your grandfather was a roaring drunk, and then your aunt Nastásya ran off with that architect.

LOMOV: And your Mother was a hunchback! *(Clutches his heart.)* Twinge, sharp pain in my side! My temples. Water!

CHUBUKOV: And then of course your father gambled away everything he had and gorged himself like a hog!

NATALYA STEPANOVNA: And your aunt could gossip to beat the band!

LOMOV: Excuse me! My left leg has gone numb! *(To CHUBUKOV.)* And as for you. . .you traitor! Oh my God my heart! It's no secret that before the last elections. . .I'm seeing stars. . .Where is my hat?

NATALYA STEPANOVNA: Lowdown snake in the grass!

CHUBUKOV: Two-faced backstabber!

LOMOV: Here it is. . .my hat. My heart! Which way! The door? I think I'm dying! Can't feel my leg!

CHUBUKOV *(pushing him toward the door)*: And I don't want to see hide or hair of you on my land again!

NATALYA STEPANOVNA *(shouting after LOMOV)*: See you in court! Sue us!

(LOMOV staggers out.)

CHUBUKOV *(pacing furiously)*: To hell with him!

NATALYA STEPANOVNA: The scoundrel. What a good neighbor!

CHUBUKOV: The bastard! Pea-brained scarecrow!

NATALYA STEPANOVNA: The freak! First, he tries to take our land, and then he turns around and calls you names!

CHUBUKOV: And you know what else? This troll. . .this little mole has the gall to come in here and propose! To propose!

NATALYA STEPANOVNA: What do you mean, propose?

CHUBUKOV: What do I mean? I mean he came over here to propose to you.

NATALYA STEPANOVNA: To Propose? To me? Why didn't you tell me before?

CHUBUKOV: Got all up in tails to do it too! The stuffed sausage! The little mushroom!

NATALYA STEPANOVNA: Propose? To me? *(Falls into the nearest armchair.)* Get him back!

CHUBUKOV: What?

NATALYA STEPANOVNA: Get him back! Ah! Get him back!

CHUBUKOV: But. . .

NATALYA STEPANOVNA *(in hysterics)*: Hurry! Hurry! I'm sick! Get him back!

CHUBUKOV: What is it? What is with you? *(Puts his hands to his head.)* Such misfortune! I'll shoot myself! I'll hang myself! This is torture!

NATALYA STEPANOVNA: I'm dying! Get him back!

CHUBUKOV: Yes! Right now! Stop howling!

(CHUBUKOV runs out.)

NATALYA STEPANOVNA *(wailing)*: What have you done! Get him back! Get him back!

CHUBUKOV *(rushes in)*: He's coming, and so on. Damn him! Talk to him yourself. I'm done with him.

NATALYA STEPANOVNA *(moaning)*: Get him back!

CHUBUKOV *(shouts)*: I *told* you, he's on his way! "Oh what a burden, my Creator, to be the father of a grown-up daughter!"[4] I'll cut my throat. I swear I will! We cursed the man, abused him, threw him out! You just couldn't keep your mouth shut!

NATALYA STEPANOVNA: Oh! And who called his father a hog?

CHUBUKOV: That's right, turn it around! I'm the one to blame!

(LOMOV appears at the door.)

CHUBUKOV: Talk to him yourself!

(CHUBUKOV leaves.)

LOMOV *(entering, exhausted)*: Horrible palpitations. . . Leg's numb . . .Twinge in my side. . .

NATALYA STEPANOVNA: Forgive me. . .forgive me! We were wrong, Ivan Vasilyevich. I remember now. . .The Little Ox Meadows are yours!

LOMOV: My heart's pounding. . .the Meadows. . . mine. . . my eyelids are twitching. . .

NATALYA STEPANOVNA: Yes yours. . .all yours! *Your* Ox Meadows. Sit down, Ivan Vasilyevich. . .sit down.

(They sit.)

---

4 Chubukov utters the final line from the Russian verse comedy *Woe from Wit* (1824) by Alexander Sergeyevich Griboyedov.

LOMOV: I. . .I acted out of principle. . .I don't care, you know, about the Ox Meadows. I don't care about the land, but just the. . .

NATALYA STEPANOVNA: . . .*principle*, yes. Now, let's you and I talk about something else.

LOMOV: And what's more is I have evidence. My aunt's grandmother gave your father's grandfather's peasants. . .

NATALYA STEPANOVNA: Yes, yes. *(To audience.)* Where do I start? *(Back to LOMOV.)* So. . .are you going hunting this season?

LOMOV: Oh yes. For black grouse, dear Natalya Stepanovna.

NATALYA STEPANOVNA: Oh!

LOMOV: After the harvest, you know. But it won't be the same this year. Have you heard? It's tragic. My dog, you know him, Cracker? Well. . .he went lame.

NATALYA STEPANOVNA: Oh no, Ivan Vasilyevich. How?

LOMOV: I don't know. . .must've twisted his paw or something. Maybe one of the other dogs bit him. *(Sighs.)* My best dog. Not to mention what I paid for him. You know I paid old Mirónov a hundred and twenty-five rubles for him.

NATALYA STEPANOVNA: You paid too much, Ivan Vasilyevich!

LOMOV: I thought it was a bargain. Fine animal.

NATALYA STEPANOVNA: Well, you know, Papa only paid eighty-five rubles for Clipper, and he's a far better dog than Cracker.

LOMOV: Clipper better than Cracker? What are you talking about? *(Laughs.)* Clipper better than Cracker.

NATALYA STEPANOVNA: Of course! I mean, I know Clipper's still a pup, but in pedigree and performance there's not a dog can touch him— even in Volchanyévsky's kennel.

LOMOV: Forgive me, Natalya Stepanovna, but you're forgetting one point. He has an overshot jaw and a weak bite.

NATALYA STEPANOVNA: A weak bite? Well that's news to me.

LOMOV: I promise. His lower jaw is shorter than the upper.

NATALYA STEPANOVNA: So you've measured it?

LOMOV: Yes, I've measured it. Now he's fine at chasing, but when it comes to catching, well he couldn't catch a. . .

NATALYA STEPANOVNA *(interrupting)*: In the first place, our Clipper is a purebred. He's the son of Gripper and Tracker. Whereas God knows what gave birth to your crossbred beast. And in the second place, your dog's older than dirt and more broken down than an old nag.

LOMOV: He may be old, but I wouldn't trade him for five of your Clippers. Cracker, now he's a *real* dog. Whereas Clipper's a. . .well, it's laughable to even try to compare. It's ridiculous. Twenty-five rubles would be a crime to charge for your Clipper.

NATALYA STEPANOVNA: A demon of contradiction has gotten into you today, Ivan Vasilyevich. First you say that the Little Ox Meadow is yours, and now Cracker is better than Clipper. I can't stand a man who won't admit the truth. You know perfectly well that Clipper is a hundred times better than your stupid Cracker. So why say the opposite?

LOMOV: Natalya Stepanovna, you must think I'm either blind or a fool. Don't you see that Clipper has an overshot jaw?

NATALYA STEPANOVNA: That's a lie.

LOMOV: He's overshot.

NATALYA STEPANOVNA *(shouts)*: Not true!

LOMOV: Why are you shouting, Madam?

NATALYA STEPANOVNA: Why are you talking nonsense? It's crazy!

NATALYA STEPANOVNA *(cont'd)*: Cracker should be shot, and you compare him to Clipper?

LOMOV: Excuse me, I cannot continue this conversation because I'm having palpitations!

NATALYA STEPANOVNA: You know, I've noticed that hunters who argue the most are the ones who understand the least.

LOMOV: Madam, will you please shut up. . .I think I'm about to have a heart attack. . . *(Shouts.)* Shut up!

NATALYA STEPANOVNA: I won't shut up until you admit that Clipper is a hundred times better than Cracker!

LOMOV: He's a hundred times worse! And I hope your Clipper drops dead! My head. . .the eyes. . .shoulder. . .

NATALYA STEPANOVNA: Well there's no need to wish your sorry dog dead, because he already looks dead!

LOMOV *(near tears)*: Shut up! I'm having a heart attack!

NATALYA STEPANOVNA: I'll never shut up!

(CHUBUKOV enters.)

CHUBUKOV: Now what's happening!

NATALYA STEPANOVNA: Papa! Just say it plain: which dog is better, our Clipper or his Cracker?

LOMOV: Stepan Stepanich! I beg you, just tell us one thing: does your Clipper have an overshot jaw? Yes or no?

CHUBUKOV: So what if he does? Who cares? He's still the best dog in the district and so on. . .

LOMOV: But my Cracker is a better dog, yes? Be honest!

CHUBUKOV: Now just hold your horses, dear boy. . .Cracker does have his good points, truly. He's purebred, firm on his feet, powerful build and so on. . .But, if you really want to know, he has two problems: he's old, and he's got a flat muzzle.

Lomov: I'm having palpitations. . .All right. Now. Let's just take a look at the *facts*. Remember, if you will. . .sir, remember at Marúskin's Field, Cracker ran neck and neck with the Count's Fury. And, if memory serves me, I believe it was Clipper who was half a mile behind.

Chubukov: That's right. The dog was behind. But that's because the Count's huntsman smacked him with a riding whip.

Lomov: Yes, yes. Now why was that? Oh yes! I believe it was because all the other dogs were chasing a fox, while your mighty Clipper went after a sheep!

Chubukov: That's not true! My dear boy, don't forget that I have a short temper, so let's stop arguing this minute. The man hit him because everyone is jealous of his neighbor's dog. And you, sir, are just like the rest. You notice someone's dog is superior to your Cracker and then you start to *needle* and so on. I remember it all!

Lomov: So do I!

Natalya Stepanovna *(mimicking)***:** "So do I!" What do you remember?

Lomov: My palpitations. . .Leg's gone numb. I can't. . .I can't . . .

Natalya Stepanovna *(mimicking again)***:** "My palpitations!". . . You're not even half a hunter! You're like a peasant. Just go back to your hut and sleep over your kitchen stove and crush cockroaches while you're at it. You shouldn't be hunting foxes! "My palpitations. . ."

Chubukov: You call yourself a hunter? You better go home and nurse those palpitations instead, boy. You might hurt yourself on a horse! Fine hunter, you are. The only reason you hunt is to pick fights with people and then pick on their dogs, and so on. I'm losing my patience, so let's drop it. You're no hunter.

Lomov: Oh, and you think you're a hunter?

Lomov *(cont'd)*: The only reason you hoist your rear-end up on a horse is to suck up to the Count and get on with your scheming. . .My heart!. . . You back stabber!

Chubukov: Back stabber? *(Shouts.)* You'd best shut up right now!

Lomov: Back stabber!

Chubukov: Whelp!

Lomov: Back-stabbing old rat!

Chubukov: Cut it out, or I'll get my gun and pick you off like a partridge!

Lomov: And we all know—Ah! My heart—that your late wife used to beat you. . .My leg. . .head . . . I see stars. . .I can't stand . . .I'm falling . . .

Chubukov: Well we all know that your housemaid keeps you on a short leash!

Lomov: I'm, I'm, I'm. . .having a heart attack! My shoulder's gone! Where's my shoulder?. . .I'm dying! *(Drops into an armchair.)* Call for a doctor!

(Lomov faints.)

Chubukov *(going for a drink of water)*: Backed down, eh? Little Gopher! Oughtta step on you! Makes me sick! *(Drinks.)* Sick!

Natalya Stepanovna: What a hunter you are! You don't know the first thing about riding a horse. *(Pause.)* Papa. . . Papa what's wrong with him? *(Pause. She shrieks.)* Papa, look! *(Screams.)* Ivan Vasilyevich. He's dead! Ivan Vasilyevich!

Chubukov: Makes me sick. . .can hardly breathe. . .need to get some air!

Natalya Stepanovna: He's dead! *(Tugs at Lomov's sleeve.)* Ivan Vasilyevich! Ivan Vasilyevich! What have we done! He's dead! *(Verging on hysteria.)* Get a doctor, a doctor!

CHUBUKOV: What is it now? What's the matter?

NATALYA STEPANOVNA *(wails)*: He's dead, he's dead!

CHUBUKOV *(going to LOMOV)*: Who's dead? Oh now. . .
(Checks the body.) He *is* dead. Mother of God! Water! Get a
doctor!

(CHUBUKOV holds a tumbler of water to LOMOV'S mouth.)

CHUBUKOV: Drink, God in Heaven *drink! (LOMOV does not
respond.)* He's not drinking. . .he's really dead and so on. .
.What misfortune! I should've ended it, put a bullet through
my brain! Why haven't I cut my throat! Why am I waiting?
Bring me a knife! Bring me a gun!

(LOMOV moves.)

CHUBUKOV: Oh look, he's coming around. Drink some
water. . .that's right my boy. . .

LOMOV: Stars. . .mist. . .Where am I?

CHUBUKOV: Oh just hurry up and marry her and to hell with
it! She says yes, boy, she says yes! *(He puts LOMOV'S hand into
his daughter's.)* The answer is yes, and so on. . .You have my
blessing! Just leave me in peace!

LOMOV *(getting to his feet)*: Hm? What? Who?

CHUBUKOV: She says yes!

NATALYA STEPANOVNA: Yes! Yes! I'll marry you! You're
alive, you're alive!

CHUBUKOV: Just kiss each other!

(They kiss.)

LOMOV: Oh, very nice. . .What's happening? What's all this
about? Oh, yes, I remember. . . my heart, and then there were
stars, but. . .but I'm very happy Natalya Stepanovna, oh yes!
Very happy! *(Kisses her hand.)* My leg is numb. . .

NATALYA STEPANOVNA: And I'm happy too!

CHUBUKOV: And it's a load off my back. . .

NATALYA STEPANOVNA *(to LOMOV)*: Now you can admit that Cracker's not as good Clipper.

LOMOV: No, he's better.

NATALYA STEPANOVNA: No he's not.

LOMOV: He's better.

NATALYA STEPANOVNA: He's worse, worse, worse!

CHUBUKOV *(trying to talk over them)*: Champagne! Champagne!

CURTAIN

R. Andrew White

Thieves

a play

from the short story of the same title
by Anton Chekhov

as translated by R. Andrew White

CHARACTERS

YERGÚNOV, a young hospital assistant

LYÚBKA, a young woman

KALÁSHNIKOV, a horse stealer, peasant

MÉRIK, a horse stealer, peasant

SETTING

Rooms in Andréi Chírikov's Inn.

R. Andrew White

Thieves

from the short story of the same title
by Anton Chekhov

as translated by R. Andrew White

Scene One

(Darkness. The sound of a raging blizzard. Dogs bark. A horse whinnies. Warm lights come up to reveal the front room of Andréi Chírikov's Inn. The blizzard persists outside. LYUBKA appears from the shadows carrying a lamp, which she places on a table. She is young, perhaps not yet twenty. YERGUNOV pounds his fist violently against the exterior of the front door. LYUBKA cautiously approaches the door.)

LYUBKA: Who's there?

YERGUNOV: Yergunov. My name is Yergunov. Let me in!

(She doesn't.)

YERGUNOV: Open the door! I need to get *warm!* For God's sake, *please!*

(Pause.)

YERGUNOV: You don't need to be afraid, old woman. I'm one of your own people!

LYUBKA: All of "my own people" are at home.

YERGUNOV: I'll die!

(She opens the door. The wind rages. YERGUNOV is inside. He is bundled up in heavy, wet winter clothing. He carries a saddle and a medical satchel. LYUBKA shuts the door and bolts it.)

LYUBKA: And I am *not* an old woman!

YERGUNOV *(pause)*: So I see. *(Beat.)* Had to tie my horse up in your stable. No workers to help me.

LYUBKA: What workers at this hour? Some are drunk and passed out, and others went to Repíno until the morning. It's a holiday. Put your things down.

(He does.)

YERGUNOV *(looks around and sees a saddle)*: That's the saddle of a Cossack.

LYUBKA: Belongs to Kalashnikov. Ever met him?

YERGUNOV: I've seen him at the hospital more than once.

LYUBKA: Well, he's at the table in the back room.

YERGUNOV: It's a beautiful saddle.

LYUBKA: He'd never settle for anything less.

(During the following, LYUBKA helps YERGUNOV take off his wet hat, gloves, coat, scarf, boots.)

YERGUNOV: Neither would I. In my line of work I couldn't afford to have second best when it comes to a horse. A medical assistant's horse, well, it's an *investment*, you know. She's beautiful—a bay mare. Not another one like her in the whole district.

LYUBKA: There isn't a horse that's a match for that blizzard. Only a fool or a drunk would be out in such weather. You picked some night to go traveling.

YERGUNOV: Had to buy supplies for the hospital. Wanted to make good time on my journey home for Christmas.

YERGUNOV *(cont'd)***:** Weather was fine when I started out, but by eight o'clock that storm swallowed me up. Must've been out there three hours. I lost my way.

LYUBKA: You certainly did.

YERGUNOV: But then I remembered. Three or four miles from the hospital is a tavern where I used to stay sometimes. And when I heard your dogs barking I knew I couldn't be far. And then I saw that red glow from your window, and the fence and the thatched roof. . .

LYUBKA: You were lucky.

YERGUNOV: Your name is Lyubka, if I remember.

LYUBKA: Lyubka, yes.

YERGUNOV: I could never forget those eyes.

(Pause.)

LYUBKA: And I could never forget the way you drink, Osíp Vasílyevich. How many nights did Papa have to drag you to the stable so you could sleep it off till morning?

YERGUNOV *(smiling)***:** Ah, yes. . .old Andréi. How's he doing?

LYUBKA: Murdered by some stagecoach drivers. Not too long ago. Beat him. Left him for dead. By the grace of God, we got him to the hospital. Died while the doctor was treating him.

(She goes to a trunk and takes out a blanket.)

YERGUNOV: I'm sure the doctor did everything he could.

LYUBKA: I guess so. *(Tosses the blanket to him.)* But I don't trust doctors.

Scene Two

(The back room of the tavern.)

(A table for dining, smaller side tables with lamps burning, a wood-burning stove, and a trunk. Near the stove are YERGUNOV's *coat, scarf, hat, and boots.* KALASHNIKOV, *a thin peasant with a silver earring sits at the table leafing through a tattered old picture book. Stretched out on the floor,* MERIK *sleeps—face, shoulders, and chest covered by a sheepskin coat.* YERGUNOV, *blanket around his shoulders, is by the stove with his saddle and the satchel warming himself. A strong wind blows against the house. The faint sound of barking dogs.)*

YERGUNOV: Some weather we're having.

(No response.)

YERGUNOV: I was up to my neck in snow, you know. Soaked to the bone, let me tell you. And with the district filled with wolves and whatnot. . .

(No response.)

YERGUNOV: Could've taken care of myself, though.

*(*YERGUNOV *pulls a revolver out of his satchel. No response.)*

YERGUNOV: Yes. Weather. . .I. . .I lost my way, and if it hadn't been for those dogs out there in the yard, I don't know what would've become of me. Would've died I should think. That would've been unpleasant.

(No response.)

YERGUNOV: Where are the women?

KALASHNIKOV: The old one went to Repíno, the young one's fixing supper.

YERGUNOV: Ah. Repíno. Just came from there myself. Had to buy some things for the hospital. That's where I work. With a lot of people. Lots and lots of people there who know me. It's nice to work with so many people who know you.

KALASHNIKOV: Yes, I know. I've been in the hospital more than once.

(Pause.)

YERGUNOV: I thought you looked familiar.

(Pause.)

KALASHNIKOV: That's a handsome saddle.

YERGUNOV: Thank you.

KALASHNIKOV: What kind of horse does it go with?

YERGUNOV: A very average bay mare. *(Beat.)* You come from Bogalyóvka, I seem to recall.

KALASHNIKOV: You have a good memory.

YERGUNOV: Well, how could one forget Bogalyóvka? Such a big village in a deep ravine. That's a treacherous ride on the way down. I remember the peasants in Bogalyóvka have a reputation for being very good—

KALASHNIKOV: Horse stealers.

YERGUNOV *(beat)*: Yes. . .I remember. But I was going to say gardeners. *(Silence.)* At any rate, I vaccinated for smallpox there once. *(Silence.)* Yes. You know, when you drive along the highroad on a moonlit night, and look down into that deep ravine and, and then up at the sky, it looks like the moon is hanging over a bottomless abyss at the end of the world.

KALASHNIKOV: That's poetic, Osíp Vasílyevich.

YERGUNOV: Ah. . .you have a good memory too!

KALASHNIKOV: I'm good with names.

YERGUNOV *(pause)*: You've been to the hospital many times.

KALASHNIKOV: Yes, in fact I was in last week to talk to the honorable doctor about horses.

YERGUNOV *(pause)*: Oh, yes?

KALASHNIKOV: To see if I could swap a dun-colored gelding for the honorable doctor's bay mare. A fine horse, that. I've had my eye on her for a long, long time. Eight years old, very quiet, still green, but she enjoys work. A very sensible animal, almost too sensible. What's her name again?

YERGUNOV: I don't remember.

KALASHNIKOV: And what a pedigree. The daughter of a sandy bay and a smoky black stallion. And that animal descended from two black horses. (Pause.) Now, my esteemed Osíp Vasílyevich, I know all the horses in this district, and I don't ever recall another bay mare.

YERGUNOV: Well. . .

KALASHNIKOV: Let us be sensible. Let's be upfront. That horse out in the stable is not your animal, is it?

(Pause.)

YERGUNOV: The honorable doctor let me borrow his horse.

KALASHNIKOV: Don't you have a horse?

YERGUNOV: No.

KALASHNIKOV: Strange.

YERGUNOV: I had to sell her. I had some debts, you see. . .

KALASHNIKOV: How does a hospital assistant work without a horse? They're always sending you God-knows-where.

YERGUNOV: I get by.

KALASHNIKOV: I'll say. You get to ride the best animal in the district! And you call the doctor's horse "very average"?

YERGUNOV: I'm not an expert on horses.

(LYUBKA enters, wearing a red dress, her hair tied in a red ribbon. She brings in a bottle of vodka with shot glasses and a plate of pickles and some sausage, which she places on the table in front of KALASHNIKOV. She is barefoot.)

LYUBKA *(to KALASHNIKOV)*: Here you go.

YERGUNOV: Hello! You look lovely.

(She notices him looking at her feet.)

LYUBKA *(on her way back to the kitchen)*: I like going barefoot when the floors have just been washed.

KALASHNIKOV *(laughing)*: Come here, little cucumber.

LYUBKA *(going to him)*: What is it?

KALASHNIKOV *(pointing in the book)*: Look here, Lyúbichka. Look at this picture. Know who that is?

LYUBKA: That's Elijah.

(KALASHNIKOV looks at her.)

LYUBKA: The prophet.

KALASHNIKOV *(of the picture)*: Now there's a man. Look how he's being pulled by three horses, straight up to the sky!

LYUBKA: They're taking him to heaven!

YERGUNOV: He didn't have to die, you know.

LYUBKA: Nope, not Elijah!

KALASHNIKOV *(still on the picture)*: Fine beasts, aren't they?

LYUBKA: The real ones were made of *fire!* You know? And so was the chariot that carried him all the way up to God.

KALASHNIKOV: Imagine. You don't have to die, and then God gives you three horses. *(To YERGUNOV.)* No need to steal them. *(Pause.)* I'm sure he turned a fine profit off those animals!

YERGUNOV: Well. . .I don't think he got to keep them.

LYUBKA: What do you mean? He didn't just *borrow* them. They were a *gift.*

(A long, plaintive moaning sound comes from the stove.)

LYUBKA: The unclean spirits are out tonight!

YERGUNOV: Sounds like a dog strangling a rat!

LYUBKA: Don't worry. It isn't the devil coming after you!

YERGUNOV: It's just the wind coming through the stove.

KALASHNIKOV: Shut up and drink.

YERGUNOV: I really shouldn't. . .not tonight. . .

(KALASHNIKOV pours out a shot for himself, and places the bottle in front of YERGUNOV, who, after a moment, pours himself a shot. They drink and each chases it with a pickle. Throughout the following, LYUBKA sets the table with a spread of food, which she brings out at different times, such as bacon, cucumbers, cheese, bread, boiled meat cut up into small pieces, or a sizzling frying pan of sausages and cabbage. When finished, she sits next to YERGUNOV— very close to him, making physical contact numerous times—maybe by accident, maybe on purpose.)

KALASHNIKOV: And what is your learned opinion, esteemed Osíp Vasílyevich? Are there devils in the world?

(YERGUNOV pours himself a second shot and throws it back, chases it with a piece of sausage.)

YERGUNOV: Well. What can I say, brother? Well. We could reason from science, I should say, that devils could not exist, for they are nothing but superstition. But if you look at it, I mean really look at it, simply, as you and I do right now, devils do exist. *(Pause.)* I have seen many in my life. When I graduated from the university, I went out to serve my medical internship in the army. I was in Turkey. I've seen war. Been decorated by the Red Cross. I have a medal. I've been out in the world, tossed here and there, so to speak. Seen more than most men can only dream of. And I have seen devils, my friend, I've seen the Devil himself. But the kind I'm talking about doesn't have horns and a tail.

Thieves

KALASHNIKOV: And where did you see him?

YERGUNOV: Met him last year. Not far from this very inn. Was on my way to Golyshíno to vaccinate for smallpox. I'm in my carriage, horse is at a nice steady trot, got all my equipment on hand, and my gold watch. I was on guard, believe me, I rode in fear the entire way. Thieves are everywhere. I come to Snake Valley. Very steep going down into that ravine. Narrow road. But I had to press on, you see, I had no choice. I began to descend, and damn it if someone doesn't come running out of the brush. You should have seen him. Black hair, the blackest eyes, his whole face smeared in soot. Here he comes right up to my animal, grabs the left rein and says "Stop!" He looks the horse up and down, and then he looks at me and drops the rein. "Where you going?" he says, and bares his teeth in this wicked grin. "I'm going to vaccinate," I tell him, "for smallpox." He casts this spiteful gaze on me, rolls up his sleeve and shoves his bare arm right under my nose. Well, I didn't want to argue with the man, so I just vaccinated him right there. But after he ran off, I looked down at my needle—it had gone rusty!

(MERIK suddenly throws off the sheepskin and leaps to his feet. Like KALASHNIKOV, he is a peasant, but he has a darker complexion. His clothing suggests that of a gypsy.)

MERIK: Aaaaah!

(YERGUNOV screams and leaps back in terror. LYUBKA squeals, and then bursts out in laughter.)

LYUBKA: Oh, Merik!

MERIK: That's what you get for conjuring the Devil! *(To YERGUNOV:)* That's quite a story you have there, hospital assistant Yergunov, but that's not how it went.

(MERIK and YERGUNOV look at one another for a moment.)

YERGUNOV: What do you mean?

MERIK: I did grab the rein, that's true. But that part about the vaccine is a lie. Soon as I had one look at that sorry nag of yours, I ran as fast as I could in the other direction!

MERIK *(cont'd)***:** My mother brings home better horses!

(KALASHNIKOV laughs.)

YERGUNOV: I'm not talking about you. Go lie down again.

KALASHNIKOV: Merik, you're mistaken. Our esteemed Osíp Vasílyevich has brought home the finest animal in the district—the honorable doctor's bay mare!

MERIK: The doctor's?

KALASHNIKOV: The very one!

MERIK: Turned to horse stealing instead of doctoring have you, Osip Vasilyevich?

YERGUNOV: I'm borrowing her.

MERIK: For a leisurely ride in the blizzard?

YERGUNOV: I had to get home. . .for the Christmas holiday . . .

(Pause.)

MERIK: Have more vodka.

(He pours a shot. YERGUNOV smiles and takes it, followed by a piece of sausage.)

MERIK: So you got rid of that sway-backed nag?

KALASHNIKOV: Sold her to pay off debts.

MERIK: You're lucky you found a buyer. She probably dropped dead the minute he got her home.

(MERIK and KALASHNIKOV laugh.)

YERGUNOV *(to MERIK)***:** I don't think I've ever seen you at the hospital.

MERIK: I don't trust doctors.

YERGUNOV: Well, let's have a drink, and a good meal, and some good conversation, eh?

(MERIK stretches and yawns and goes over to sit next to LYUBKA and KALASHNIKOV.)

LYUBKA *(pointing to the book)*: Merik, if you got me horses like these, I'd ride all the way to heaven with you!

MERIK *(putting his arm around LYUBKA)*: They don't let people like us in.

(LYUBKA gets up and begins clearing a couple of empty plates. YERGUNOV watches her. MERIK watches YERGUNOV and pours himself a shot.)

LYUBKA: I'd get in.

KALASHNIKOV: Sinners can't ride into heaven. Heaven is for the holy.

(YERGUNOV takes some more sausage, and indicates that he would like another shot. MERIK happily pours him one.)

MERIK: Lyubka, bring in a bottle of that dark vodka for our guest.

(On her way out LYUBKA lovingly swats MERIK on the back of the head with her free hand.)

MERIK *(to YERGUNOV)*: I saw you eyeing our Lyubichka.

(Pause.)

YERGUNOV: Are you and she, uh. . .

MERIK: Yes.

(LYUBKA enters and puts the bottle of dark vodka on the table. She clears any empty plates.)

YERGUNOV: Lyubka, don't you ever sit still? You're here and there. You're like a fidgety child.

(LYUBKA brushes her body against YERGUNOV—maybe by accident, maybe on purpose.)

LYUBKA *(her face close to his)*: I can be still when I die.

KALASHNIKOV: Unless you go out like that Elijah.

LYUBKA: Only God's favorites get to go out in a blaze of fire like that. *(Beat. To YERGUNOV.)* You ate all the sausage!

(She brushes against YERGUNOV again as she collects the empty plate. She continues clearing and/or setting the table with food during the following.)

YERGUNOV: Here, let's have one more shot.

MERIK: I've had enough.

KALASHNIKOV: So have I.

YERGUNOV: Well. . .I never drink alone, but just one more.

(MERIK pours out a healthy shot of the dark vodka, which YERGUNOV drinks and chases with food.)

YERGUNOV: Now, you all in Bogalyóvka. . .

KALASHNIKOV: . . .yes. . .

YERGUNOV: . . .you're a fine bunch of folks.

KALASHNIKOV: How do you mean?

YERGUNOV *(to MERIK)***:** My friend and I, here, we were talking while you were asleep, about how the peasants in Bogalyóvka have a reputation for being horse stealers. . .

KALASHNIKOV *(to MERIK)***:** Nowadays, they're just a bunch of drunks and robbers.

MERIK *(to KALASHNIKOV)***:** The only real horse stealer left is old Fílya, and he's half blind.

KALASHNIKOV: Yes, no one but Fílya. He must be pushing seventy by now. A dying breed. . .

(KALASHNIKOV and MERIK ignore YERGUNOV as they continue to talk.)

KALASHNIKOV: Remember what he did with Lyubka's father?

MERIK: Andréi Grigóryevich! God rest his soul.

KALASHNIKOV: Yes! Stole off one night where some cavalry regiments were stationed. They made off with nine soldiers' horses!

MERIK: The very best of them!

YERGUNOV: With Lyubka's father?

KALASHNIKOV: *Nine soldiers!* The sentry didn't scare them one bit. Next morning they sold every last one of those horses for twenty rubles to that gypsy.

YERGUNOV: What was his name?

(Pause. MERIK and KALASHNIKOV look at YERGUNOV.)

MERIK: You don't belong here. *(Pause.)* His name was Afónka.

(Beat.)

KALASHNIKOV: But today what do we have? A man only steals a horse while the rider is drunk or asleep. *(He spits.)* Then he slinks off, goes a hundred miles away and haggles at the market place till the police catch him. They're all fools. It's disgusting!

LYUBKA: But what about Merik?

KALASHNIKOV: He's not from Bogalyóvka. He's a Khárkov man from Mezhýrich. A fearless man and that's the truth. He's a good man.

LYUBKA: It wasn't for nothing that all of his good people gave him a bath in that hole they cut in the ice!

YERGUNOV: How was that?

LYUBKA: Tell him, Merik, tell him!!

MERIK *(looks at YERGUNOV; decides to tell the story)*: Well . . .it was like this. Fílya, he carried off three horses from a workers' camp at Samolyénka. Must've been about thirty tenants there altogether. So it turns out one of 'em sees us at the market. The man comes up to me, taps me on the shoulder. "Come here. I got some horses to show you.

MERIK *(cont'd)***:** We bought 'em from the fair!" Of course I'm interested, so I follow this man, and then all *thirty* of 'em are standing there, and they jump me, tie my hands behind my back, and lead me to the river. "We'll show you some horses!" they say. Now there were two holes in the river ice. They'd already cut one, and then about seven feet away they cut another. Then, you know, they tie a rope into a noose under my armpits, and at the other end they tie a crooked stick so that it would, you know, reach from one hole to the other. So, they put the stick under the ice and pull it through the holes. Then, they shove me into the hole in the ice—fur coat, high boots and all! And they stand there and jab me, one with his foot, another with a heavy *axe*. Finally, they drag me under the ice and pull me up through the other hole.

(LYUBKA giggles and claps.)

MERIK: I thought I was a dead man. When they pulled me out, I was helpless and lay in the snow, and they all stood around me and beat me with sticks and kicked me in my knees and in my gut. Hurt like hell. Then they went away ...and everything on me was frozen, my blood, my clothes were icing over. I tried to stand, but I couldn't. Thank God an old woman drove by and gave me a ride.

YERGUNOV: I got one for you. I'll tell you what happened to me in Penza—

KALASHNIKOV: The kingdom of heaven and never ending peace to Lyubka's dear father, Andréi Grigóryevich.

(He pours out two shots of the dark vodka and clinks glasses with MERIK. LYUBKA finishes clearing the table and exits.)

KALASHNIKOV: When he was alive—

YERGUNOV: To Andréi Grigóryevich.

(MERIK and KALASHNIKOV look at each other. A moment. MERIK pours out a shot for YERGUNOV, who drinks. There is no food left to chase it.)

(LYUBKA runs in wearing a green kerchief and a string of beads.)

LYUBKA: Look, Merik. Look what Kalashnikov brought me today! And you won't believe the treasures I have! Look at this.

(She opens the trunk and begins to take out articles of clothing. KALASHNIKOV picks up a guitar and plays. LYUBKA takes out a hand mirror, looks at her reflection and shakes her head several times to make the beads jingle.)

LYUBKA: Look. A cotton dress with red and blue dots!

MERIK: Well, well. . .

LYUBKA: And a red one with fringe, a new handkerchief. This bracelet and more beads. . .

MERIK: Kalashnikov, I had no idea you were so generous! *(Leaps out of his seat.)* But now I'm stealing the goods!

(He grabs LYUBKA, who laughs, and begins to dance wildly with her as KALASHNIKOV continues to play the guitar. He buries his face in her neck and hair and sniffs loudly.)

MERIK: You smell of soap!

LYUBKA *(laughing)*: Stop! *Stop!* Your whiskers. . .

(MERIK spins LYUBKA and lets her go. He pounds his heels into the floor standing in one place. Then he squats and begins dancing all around the room. LYUBKA shrieks gleefully, throws the green kerchief to the floor, letting her hair billow freely, and follows him, tapping the floor with her bare heels. YERGUNOV watches the whole time. As LYUBKA passes him, she caresses his face and tosses a scarf over his head. YERGUNOV slams down one more shot. He yells, stands up and takes LYUBKA in his arms and dances with her. MERIK rushes over and shoves YERGUNOV away from LYUBKA.)

MERIK: Hands off! This is a *peasant* song!

(KALASHNIKOV stops playing.)

MERIK: I know what you're thinking.

YERGUNOV: Now, wait. . . I—

MERIK: But you're not one of us. Do you hear? *(Pause.)*
You're not one of us.

YERGUNOV *(sitting)***:** Yes. . .yes, I know.

(Silence.)

MERIK *(to KALASHNIKOV)***:** Play.

*(KALASHNIKOV plays, and MERIK spins LYUBKA and the two
dance. At last they stop, and LYUBKA sinks into his chest,
leaning against him, exhausted. He puts his arms around
her. They are both breathing heavily. MERIK caresses her
softly.)*

MERIK *(tenderly, affectionately, as if joking)***:** I'll find out
where your old mother hides her money, I'll kill her, and I'll
cut your little throat with a knife, and after that I'll set the
inn on fire. . .People will think you died in the fire, and I'll
go to Kubán with your money and keep herds of horses and
flocks of sheep. . .

LYUBKA: Is it nice in Kubán, Merik?

(He lets go of her and goes to sit on the trunk.)

KALASHNIKOV: It's time for me to go. Fílya must be waiting
for me. Good night Lyubka. Good night, Merik, my brother.
(To YERGUNOV.) Be careful of those devils. Remember,
thieves are everywhere!

*(KALASHNIKOV goes. After a moment, YERGUNOV gets up and
follows KALASHNIKOV. A moment. LYUBKA goes to MERIK. A
kiss.)*

MERIK: I'll be in your room.

*(He exits. After a moment, YERGUNOV returns. LYUBKA looks
at him.)*

LYUBKA: Worried?

YERGUNOV: No. I watched him. He left on his own horse. As soon as he set out, that short-legged little horse of his was up to her belly in a snowdrift. He was white all over with snow. They vanished.

(Silence. YERGUNOV pours another shot.)

YERGUNOV: Drink?

LYUBKA: No thank you.

(Through the following, YERGUNOV watches LYUBKA as she puts her belongings back into the trunk and then goes about the room extinguishing lanterns until only one is left burning.)

YERGUNOV: So. . .will Merik spend the night?

LYUBKA: Why do you ask?

(YERGUNOV picks up the scarf she tossed onto his face.)

YERGUNOV: "Hands off," he said, "this is a peasant song. You're not one of us." *(Beat.)* You know, I've been sitting here all night with my thoughts all. . .tangled, and I'm just thinking, what's the difference, you know? Who is he to say that anyway? *(Beat.)* I mean why in the world must we have doctors, medical assistants, merchants, clerks and peasants? Everyone "with his own people"? What's wrong with just having simple, free people? Huh? Aren't birds free? Aren't the animals free? They're not afraid of anything and don't need anyone! Isn't Merik free? Just listen to him when he talks. *(Pause.)* And, by the way, whose idea was it, who deemed it necessary that people must get up in the morning, eat lunch at noon, go to bed at night. Look at me! Do you ever think of that? Who was it decided that a doctor is more important than a medical assistant, that you have to live in a room and love only your wife? Why not the other way around? Lunch at night and sleep during the day? Ah, to jump on a horse without asking who owned it, to ride like the devil and run races with the wind through fields, forests, and ravines, to make love to girls, to laugh at everyone. . . Why is it a sin to enjoy yourself, Lyubka?

YERGUNOV *(cont'd)***:** Do you like to enjoy yourself? Those of us, Lyubka. . .those people who live without freedom, they have been beggars all their lives. They live without pleasure. They go home at night. They go to work in the morning. They are faithful to their wives, who are like frogs. *(Beat.)* I've never been a thief, I'm not a swindler. I've never taken anything away from anyone. *(Touches LYUBKA.)* But you know what? I've never had a good opportunity. To take. To just take what I want when I want. *(Pause.)*

LYUBKA: Give me the scarf.

(YERGUNOV does. As LYUBKA exits, she brushes up against him. Maybe by accident, maybe on purpose.)

YERGUNOV: You're a flame of a girl. You may only be a girl, but you're no virgin. Even if you were. . .why should I be a gentleman in a den of thieves?

(YERGUNOV finds the blanket that LYUBKA gave him and spreads it out by the stove. LYUBKA's laughter off stage.)

MERIK *(off)***:** C'mere.

LYUBKA *(off)***:** Merik. . .

(Her laughter subsides.)

YERGUNOV: If only the unclean spirits would take Merik away.

(He blows out the lamp.)

Scene Three

(The back room. Early morning light. Outside, the wind has subsided. YERGUNOV sleeps on the floor near the stove. MERIK enters wearing his sheepskin coat. He moves swiftly but quietly. LYUBKA enters, following him.)

LYUBKA: Merik!

MERIK: Shh!

LYUBKA: Stay! I love you.

MERIK: No, Lyubka, don't keep me!

LYUBKA: Listen to me. I know that you'll find Mama's money, and destroy her and me, and go to Kubán and make love to other girls, and God be with you. But I ask only one thing, dear heart—stay!

MERIK: No, I want to be free.

LYUBKA: How are you going to get to Kubán? You walked here, what are you going to ride?

(MERIK leans in close and whispers in LYUBKA'S ear. She laughs through her tears.)

LYUBKA *(looking at YERGUNOV)*: And he's still asleep, the pompous Satan.

MERIK: He was so drunk last night, he'll probably sleep till sunset.

(MERIK kisses her hard and exits. A moment, and YERGUNOV jumps up, revolver in hand, and starts after him. LYUBKA moves quickly in front of him.)

YERGUNOV: Get out of my way!

(He tries to pass.)

LYUBKA: Why do you want to go out?

YERGUNOV: To look after my horse.

(LYUBKA looks him up and down, slyly and affectionately.)

LYUBKA: Why look at a horse? Wouldn't you rather look at me?

(She delicately touches his chest.)

YERGUNOV: Let me out, or he'll ride off with my horse.

(LYUBKA runs her hand down to his belt buckle.)

LYUBKA: She isn't your horse.

(LYUBKA begins kissing his neck.)

Yergunov: Let me go. He'll ride away, I'm telling you. . .

Lyubka: Where to? He won't leave.

Yergunov: I have to. . .

Lyubka: Have to what?

(He starts to go.)

Lyubka: Don't go, dear heart. I'll get bored all by myself.

Yergunov: Don't play games with me. . .

Lyubka: We'll ride together to heaven, yes?

(She kisses his neck.)

Yergunov: I heard you tell Merik just now that you loved him.

Lyubka: So what. . .in my heart I know who I love.

(Beat. He kisses her hard. Offstage, the faint sound of a horse whinny. He pulls away, and tries to go.)

Lyubka: No. Stay. Now you can take. Take anything you want, when you want. . .

(He kisses her again, and Lyubka grabs for the gun, which he still holds.)

Yergunov: No!

(He pushes her aside and runs out. Lyubka watches after him for a moment. Then, seeing his saddle on the floor, picks it up and places it on top of the trunk. She runs her hands gently over the saddle, caressing it. Yergunov runs back inside.)

Yergunov: Where did he go? *(No answer.)* Where? *(No answer.)* Answer me, you devil! You tell me where he's going with that horse, or I'll kick the life out of you.

(He moves toward her.)

Lyubka: Get away you *filth!*

*(YERGUNOV grabs her, and then kisses her viciously. LYUBKA
breaks free and strikes him a heavy blow to the head.
YERGUNOV staggers and drops his gun. He reaches for her
again. She delivers another fierce blow and runs out. He
begins to lose consciousness. As he slowly goes down to the
floor, the morning light slowly fades to darkness.
YERGUNOV remains in a dim pool of light. Winter wind
blows.)*

Epilogue

*(YERGUNOV lay in the pool of light. Gradually, the sound of
the wind transforms into the sound of crickets chirping
and of a spring night. YERGUNOV slowly presses himself up
and sits. He looks up.)*

YERGUNOV: My God, how vast the stars, how deep the sky,
and how wide it stretches over the world.

*(He reaches into his pocket and takes out a box of matches.
He lights one.)*

YERGUNOV: One. *(Lights another.)* Two. *(Lights another.)*
Three. *(Another.)* Four. Why do people divide each other
into the sober and the drunk, the employed and the jobless?

(MERIK appears.)

MERIK: You would've lost your job even if I hadn't made
away with the honorable doctor's bay mare.

YERGUNOV: A year and a half ago. . .a year and a half.
(Lights another.) Five. . . *(Lights another.)* Six. *(Another.)*
Seven *(Another.)* Eight.

(KALASHNIKOV appears.)

YERGUNOV: And why do those who are sober and eat well
sleep peacefully in their homes while the drunk and hungry
wander the fields, without shelter?

KALASHNIKOV: You should move to Bogalyóvka and keep
company with all the other drunks and petty thieves.

KALASHNIKOV *(cont'd)*: Maybe you'll get lucky and work for one-eyed Fílya.

YERGUNOV: *(Lights another.)* Nine. *(Lights another.)* Ten. *(Another.)* Eleven. *(Beat.)* Why would it be a sin if I stole a samovar yesterday to sell for a drink today?

MERIK: I stole more than "the honorable doctor's" horse, you know.

(YERGUNOV closes his eyes for a moment. He lights another match and watches it burn. He blows out the match.)

YERGUNOV: And why must those who have no work and receive no wages go hungry, naked, and shoeless?

MERIK: Look at the horizon, Osíp Vasílyevich. Toward Chirikov's Inn.

(YERGUNOV does. LYUBKA appears.)

LYUBKA: Look at the crimson glow. . .

KALASHNIKOV: . . .bursting over the horizon. . .

YERGUNOV: Why is it a sin to steal a horse from some rich man's stable?

KALASHNIKOV: . . .that's no sunset. . .

(KALASHNIKOV disappears.)

YERGUNOV: . . .riding like the devil. . .

MERIK: . . .the young one, and her old mother lying on the floor with their throats slit. . .

LYUBKA: Only God's favorites get to go out in a blaze of fire like that.

YERGUNOV: . . .running races with the wind.

MERIK: I always keep my promises.

(Pause.)

LYUBKA: Is it nice in Kubán, Merik?

MERIK: . . .herds of horses. . .flocks of sheep.

(**LYUBKA** *disappears.*)

YERGUNOV: How I envy you, Merik.

(*MERIK disappears.*)

YERGUNOV: How I envy. . .

(*Silence. YERGUNOV lights a thirteenth match and watches it burn.*)

YERGUNOV: Christ Jesus, help me.

(*He blows it out.*)

END OF PLAY

R. Andrew White

The Fiancée

a play

from the short story of the same title
by Anton Chekhov

as translated by R. Andrew White

This adaptation of *The Fiancée* was presented by Valparaiso University, Valparaiso, IN in February, 2000. It was directed by R. Andrew White. The costume designs were by Ann Kessler, and the set design was by Alan Stalmah. The cast was as follows:

NADYA SHUMINA	Meghan Bell
NINA IVANOVNA	Amber Hilgenkamp
MARFA MIKHAILOVNA	Vanessa Hughes
ANDREI ANDREICH	Justin Bayle
FATHER ANDREI	Andrew Holmes
ALEXANDER TIMOFEYICH (SASHA)	Ray Palasz
ACTOR #1	David Kelch
ACTOR #2	Deborah Craft
ACTOR #3	Paul Oren

CHARACTERS

NÁDYA SHÚMINA, a young woman, 23 years old

NÍNA IVÁNOVNA SHÚMINA, her mother; wears a *pince-nez*, a tight corset, and diamonds on every finger

MÁRFA MIKHÁILOVNA SHÚMINA, her grandmother

ANDRÉI ANDRÉICH, her fiancé

FATHER ANDRÉI, his father; a lean and toothless old man, and priest of the local cathedral

ALEXÁNDER TIMOFÉICH (SÁSHA), a friend of the family

ENSEMBLE MEMBERS assume the roles of servants who assist in scene changes and share narration, which should be distributed as appropriate for the production. If desired, the narration may be distributed among the principal characters without using an extended ensemble.

SETTING

The action takes place in various locations in a
provincial town and in Moscow. The simpler, the
better. Basic set components and furniture props
may be configured to represent a variety of areas.
The point is to keep the play flowing smoothly and
efficiently.

R. Andrew White

The Fiancée

from the short story of the same title
by Anton Chekhov

as translated by R. Andrew White

*(Lights up. An ENSEMBLE MEMBER carries a triangle and
strikes it ten times under the following.)*

ENSEMBLE: It was already ten o'clock in the evening, and a
full moon was shining over the garden.

FATHER ANDREI: In the Shumin's home, they were
finishing daily evening prayers. . .

MARFA MIKHAILOVNA: . . .which were ordered by the
grandmother of the house, Marfa Mikhailovna.

NADYA: And now Nadya, who had gone out to the garden
for a minute, could see that the table in the dining room was
being set with appetizers, and Grandmother was bustling
about in her wonderful silk dress.

NINA IVANOVNA: Nadya was already twenty-three, and
from the age of sixteen she had dreamed passionately of
marriage.

ANDREI ANDREICH: And now she was the fiancée of Andrei
Andreich. . .

FATHER ANDREI: . . .Father Andrei's son.

ANDREI ANDREICH: He was strong and handsome and looked like an actor or an artist.

(ANDREI ANDREICH takes NADYA's hands in his. He kisses her.)

NADYA: She liked him.

ENSEMBLE: Their wedding was set for July seventh.

ANDREI ANDREICH: I'm so lucky!

ENSEMBLE: From the open window of the kitchen in the basement came the sound of servants scuttling about. . .of knives clanging. . . of the door slamming on its frame. . .the aroma of roast turkey and marinated cherries was in the air.

NADYA: And for some reason it seemed to Nadya that life would always be this way, without change, without end.

(The ENSEMBLE disperses. NADYA is in the garden at night.)

NADYA: In the garden it was quiet, cool, and dark peaceful shadows lay across the ground. From somewhere far away, very far away, probably outside the town, came the sound of croaking frogs. *(She breathes deeply.)* May was in the air! Sweet, wonderful May!

(SASHA has been watching.)

SASHA: You snuck out.

NADYA: Sasha! Breathe the air! When you breathe it so deeply, you imagine that you're somewhere else, somewhere far away, where spring is starting life all over again, and for some reason (I don't know why) it makes me want to cry.

SASHA: It's nice here.

NADYA: Of course it's nice. *(Beat.)* You should wait until autumn to go back to Moscow.

(SASHA laughs. They sit.)

SASHA: I probably will. Maybe until September.

NADYA *(looking toward the house)*: Look at Mama through the window. How young she seems from out here! She has her weaknesses, I know, but she's an extraordinary woman.

SASHA: Yes, she's nice. . .in her own way, of course. . .she's very kind and sweet, but (how can I put this?) when I went down into that kitchen early this morning, I saw four servants sleeping right there *on the floor*, with a pile of rags for a bed, and some kind of stink, bedbugs, roaches. . . God! Just like it was twenty years ago—not a bit of change! As for your grandmother, well, she's set in her ways and, God bless her, she took me in, put me through school when my poor mother died.

NADYA: I'm glad you remember.

SASHA: Of course I do!

NADYA: Only took you fifteen years to earn a diploma. . .

SASHA: . . .for which I am grateful. . .

NADYA: . . .all so that you could manage a lithography shop in Moscow.

(Pause.)

SASHA: Are you finished?

(NADYA is silent.)

SASHA: As I was about to say. . .I understand that she can't change, but your mother, she speaks French fluently, is very well read, performs in community theatre. . .You'd think she would be more . . . *enlightened. (Beat.)* Everything here is just. . .it's absurd. I guess I'm not used to it anymore. Damn it, nobody does anything around here. Your mama strolls around all day like some kind of duchess, your grandma does nothing. . .and neither do you.

NADYA: (Here we go.)

SASHA: And on top of it. . .

NADYA: That will *do*.

SASHA: . . .your soon-to-be husband, Andréi Andréich, does nothing either.

NADYA: Sasha. You've been here a whole ten days and somehow, by the grace of God, you've managed to restrain yourself from repeating what you said to me last summer, and the summer before.

SASHA: I have mastered self-control.

NADYA: A small miracle. *(Beat.)* Look, I know it's the only way your mind works, but can you please come up with something new to complain about?

(SASHA laughs.)

SASHA: Look at you—tall, slender, beautiful—so healthy and elegant, so full of life.

(Awkward silence.)

NADYA: You're hopeless, and I pity you, I really do.

SASHA: And I pity your youth.

(Pause.)

MARFA MIKHAILOVNA *(off)*: Nadya!

NADYA: You say too much.

MARFA MIKHAILOVNA *(off)*: *Nadya!*

NADYA: *I'm coming! (To SASHA.)* You don't know him.

(The living room. Ensemble sets samovar, serves tea, etc. ANDREI ANDREICH, NINA IVANOVNA, MARFA MIKHAILOVNA, and FATHER ANDREI enter.)

NADYA: After supper Andréi Andréich played the violin while Mama accompanied him on the piano.

SASHA: Ten years earlier he had graduated from the university with a degree in philology, but he didn't have a job, had no real occupation and only occasionally participated in charity concerts.

NADYA *(glaring at SASHA)*: Everyone in town calls him an artist.

(They enter the scene.)

MARFA MIKHAILOVNA *(to SASHA)*: You'll fatten up after a week with us! You have to eat more. What a sickly looking, skinny thing you are. As I live and breathe, you're a real prodigal son! Every summer, he comes here to rest and recuperate. A real prodigal son.

FATHER ANDREI: He has squandered his father's wealth and was sent to feed with the senseless swine.

(Laughter.)

ANDREI ANDREICH: I love my papa! Nice old man! Good old man!

(SASHA suddenly laughs.)

FATHER ANDREI: Nina Ivanovna, I understand you believe in hypnotism.

NINA IVANOVNA: I can't confirm that I do, of course, but I must confess that there is much in nature which is mysterious and inexplicable.

FATHER ANDREI: I agree completely with you, but I'm obliged to add that faith significantly reduces for us the realm of the mysterious.

NINA IVANOVNA *(irritated)*: Well. . .of course I wouldn't dare argue with you, but you must agree that life is full of unsolved mysteries!

FATHER ANDREI: Not one, I assure you.

(An ENSEMBLE MEMBER strikes a triangle twelve times under the following.)

FATHER ANDREI: Midnight already! Well, my dear Marfa Mikhailovna, we really must be leaving.

NADYA *(To ANDREI ANDREICH)*: I'll walk you to the garden.

(NADYA and ANDREI walk. ENSEMBLE clears tea, etc. NADYA and ANDREI attempt a passionate kiss.)

ANDREI ANDREICH: I'm out of my mind with ecstasy! Goodnight.

(ANDREI ANDREICH exits.)

NADYA: After saying goodnight to her fiancé, Nadya went to her room upstairs where she lived with her mother.

ENSEMBLE *(exiting)*: The servants worked long into the night cleaning up. . .

MARFA MIKHAILOVNA *(exiting)*: . . .while Granny scolded them.

(Silence. The stage is empty except for NADYA.)

NADYA: And finally. . .*finally* there was quiet in the house.

(The sound of SASHA'S deep cough, offstage.)

NADYA: Except for the sound of Sasha coughing in his room downstairs.

(The sounds of the early morning. Crows caw in the distance. The garden. NINA IVANOVNA appears. She has been weeping.)

NADYA: Mama.

NINA IVANOVNA: Oh, good morning. Goodness, dear, you're up early.

NADYA: I couldn't sleep last night.

NINA IVANOVNA: Neither could I.

(They walk.)

NADYA: I've just been awake every night this month. My bed isn't comfortable anymore. It's too soft. I lay awake and begin to think, and I have the same thoughts night after night about Andrei Andreich and how he courted me and proposed to me, and how I have come to, to. . .

NADYA *(cont'd)*: . . .*accept* him and his kindness and intelligence. But now there's so little time before our wedding and I'm. . .Mama, I'm scared. What makes me feel like this? You know all about these things. What is it that makes me so sad?

NINA IVANOVNA: You're sad?

NADYA: Are all girls like this before their weddings? Do they all feel like I do?

NINA IVANOVNA: Well, of course dear. It's only your youth.

NADYA: Do you think so? Or is it Sasha? Because I think it might be Sasha.

NINA IVANOVNA: You're in love with Sasha?

NADYA: *No*, Mama, I mean his *influence*. But he only repeats himself. Every time he visits, he just harps on the same old thing. And I think he's very naïve. Really I do.

(Somewhere within, the sound of SASHA's harsh, nagging cough. Pause.)

NINA IVANOVNA: That boy should take better care of himself.

NADYA: But why can't I get what he says out of my head?

NINA IVANOVNA: Because he's unreasonably persistent.

(Beat.)

NADYA: Why were you crying a moment ago, Mama?

(Pause.)

NINA IVANOVNA: Last night I started reading a story about an old man and his daughter. The old man works in some office and, well, his boss falls in love with the old man's daughter. I didn't finish reading it, but I came to a place where it was difficult to keep from crying. This morning I remembered it and cried again.

(NADYA just looks at her mother.)

87

NADYA: Uh-huh.

NINA IVANOVNA: I don't know, dear, but when I can't sleep I shut my eyes tight—like this—and I imagine something historical, from the ancient world.

NADYA: Mama, you don't understand.

NINA IVANOVNA: . . .or sometimes I envision Anna Karenina. . .

NADYA: I've never felt this way, I'm frightened.

NINA IVANOVNA: I imagine the things she said. . .

NADYA: . . .*Mother*. . .

NINA IVANOVNA: . . .and the way she walked. . .

NADYA: I think I'm losing something. . .

NINA IVANOVNA: And then I feel ever so much better.

NADYA: Something inside me is dying.

NINA IVANOVNA: Yes, Anna Karenina. . .

(The sound of ANDREI ANDREICH playing the violin off stage. NINA IVANOVNA exits. The living room. SASHA enters.)

SASHA: If only you would listen to me!

NADYA: It's hard to take you seriously after all of those jokes you made over dinner. They weren't even funny!

SASHA: They weren't meant to be.

NADYA: And before every one of your "punchlines" you lifted your two boney fingers just to make sure we get the "moral of the story."

SASHA: I'm trying to enlighten you.

NADYA: Oh, thank you, *thank you* for handing down your wisdom from the mountaintop!

SASHA: That's not the point.

NADYA: And the point is?

SASHA: That you would leave this little, gray, backwater, *benighted* town and go to school! *(Pause.)* Do you know, educated people, enlightened people are the only people this world needs? And the more people who are like them, the sooner the kingdom of God will be here on earth. Then, even here, in this stagnant little village, not one stone will be stacked neatly on top of another, because everything will have been turned upside-down, everything will change as if by magic. And there will be enormous, beautiful houses here, wonderful gardens, magnificent fountains, remarkable people. . .But that isn't the main thing. The main thing is that the crowd, the unthinking crowd as we know it, this evil will no longer exist, because every person will have faith, and know what he lives for, and no one will seek support from this crowd. My dear, my darling, go! Show everyone that you're sick of this stagnant, gray, sinful life. At least show yourself!

NADYA: It's impossible, Sasha. I'm getting married.

(Violin playing stops.)

SASHA: Don't be silly! Who needs that? And, anyway, my dear, you have to think, you have to understand how impure, how immoral this idle life of yours is. Don't you understand? Since you, your mother, and granny do nothing, someone else is working for you! You are consuming someone else's life! *You* are the burden they carry! And is that pure? Isn't that poisonous?

NADYA: Nadya wanted to say, "yes, it's true," wanted to say that she understood, wanted to—

(ANDREI ANDREICH enters with his violin.)

NADYA: Andrei! Dear.

ANDREI ANDREICH: I came to say goodnight.

NADYA: Yes. Yes, of course you did. *(To SASHA.)* If you don't mind, Sasha. . .

SASHA: Goodnight. *(He goes.)*

(With violin and bow in hand, ANDREI takes NADYA in his arms, and they attempt a passionate kiss.)

ANDREI ANDREICH: Oh, my love, my life! I'm so happy, I'm out of my mind with ecstasy!

(Another kiss, and ANDREI ANDREICH steps aside.)

NADYA: And it seemed to Nadya that all of this had somehow played out before, or that she had read it in some old, ragged, long-forgotten novel.

(ENSEMBLE enters.)

ENSEMBLE: Time passed. . .Saint Peter's day. . .June twenty-ninth. . .After dinner Andrei Andreich went with Nadya to Moscow Street once again to inspect the house that had been rented and long-since prepared for the young couple. It was two stories, but so far only the top story had been furnished.

(ENSEMBLE MEMBER takes ANDREI ANDREICH'S violin as he and NADYA begin their tour of the house.)

ANDREI ANDREICH: Look how the ballroom floor shines! It's freshly painted!

NADYA: I can smell it. . .

ANDREI ANDREICH: It looks just like real parquet!

NADYA: . . .the paint fumes, I mean.

ANDREI ANDREICH: And, look, Viennese chairs. . .

NADYA: . . .a grand piano. . .

ANDREI ANDREICH: . . .and a music stand for the violin.

(They stop, and face out front. Their heads move up and down as they look at an enormous painting on the wall.)

NADYA: What a colorful picture of a naked woman.

NADYA *(cont'd):* What do you think the purple vase with the broken handle means?

(Pause.)

ANDREI ANDREICH: I think, perhaps, it symbolizes. . . *something.* It's by the artist Shishmachévsky.

NADYA: Who?

(ENSEMBLE holds an empty picture frame. FATHER ANDREI ANDREICH enters in a kamilavka—*a tall piece of headgear of Orthodox priests—and wearing decorative ribbons and medals, and poses inside the frame.)*

ENSEMBLE: Next was the living room with a round table, a sofa and armchairs upholstered in bright blue material. Over the sofa hung a large photograph of Father Andrei.

ANDREI ANDREICH: And, see, Papa's portrait!

ENSEMBLE: They went into the dining room.

NADYA: What a lovely sideboard.

ANDREI ANDREICH: And then, the bedroom.

NADYA: And in the semi-darkness stood two beds side by side, and it seemed as though the bedroom had been furnished with the assumption that it would always be very happy there, and could not be otherwise.

ANDREI ANDREICH: He escorted her through the other rooms. . .

NADYA: . . .with his arm around her waist like an iron hoop . . .

ANDREI ANDREICH: I'm so lucky!

NADYA: She felt weak, guilty, and hated every room, the beds, the armchairs. The naked lady made her feel nauseous.

ANDREI ANDREICH: *We're* so lucky!

NADYA: It was so clear to her now.

ANDREI ANDREICH: I'm out of my mind with ecstasy!

NADYA: She had fallen out of love with him, or maybe she never loved him at all.

(She begins to feel anxious.)

ANDREI ANDREICH: I've yearned so long for a place of our own.

NADYA *(her anxiety intensifies)*: And all she could see, all she could *feel* was his banality—his stupid, naïve, intolerable banality.

ANDREI ANDREICH: I love you.

NADYA *(on the verge of a panic attack)*: She was ready at any moment to flee, to begin sobbing and to throw herself out the window!

ANDREI ANDREICH: How do you like it?

NADYA *(smiling, absolutely calm)*: I think it's very nice.

ANDREI ANDREICH: And remember, yesterday, how Sasha complained that he "couldn't live in this town"? "No running water" he said. Well, I had them install a tank that holds *one hundred gallons* of water, so we will always have running water!

NADYA: Wonderful.

ANDREI ANDREICH: And *then*, you remember, Sasha criticized *me* for not doing anything. Well, you know what? He's *infinitely* right! I don't do anything. I *can't* do anything. My dear, why is that? Why am I so disgusted by the very thought of one day working in the civil service? Why do I feel so uneasy when I see a lawyer, or a Latin teacher, or a town councilor? Oh Mother Russia, how many idle and useless people you still carry! How many like me, oh long-suffering Mother Russia! Why don't I do anything?

(He looks at her.)

NADYA: Why?

ANDREI ANDREICH: It's a sign of the times. But not for long. When we get married, let's find a place in the country, my darling, where we will work! We'll buy a little plot of land with a garden, a river, and we will work and watch life go by. Oh how nice it will be!

NADYA: She listened to him and thought: "God, I just want to go home!"

(ANDREI ANDREICH exits. A strong wind howls. ENSEMBLE shifts the scene to the Shumin's Home.)

ENSEMBLE: That night the wind pounded against the windows and roof. . .a whistling could be heard, and the house goblin in the stove sang his song sullenly and plaintively. . .It was one o'clock in the morning. . .everyone in the house had gone to bed, but no one slept.

NADYA: And Nadya kept thinking she could hear someone playing the violin downstairs.

(A loud, harsh pop, almost like a gunshot.)

NINA IVANOVNA: Nadya!

(NINA IVANOVNA rushes in.)

NINA IVANOVNA: Oh, Nadya. Thank God you're all right. For a moment, I. . .What was that noise?

NADYA: I think the wind blew off one of the shutters.

NINA IVANOVNA: Oh. . .I see. . .I'll have someone look at it tomorrow. I just wanted to see that you were all right. Good night, dear.

NADYA: Goodnight.

(NINA IVANOVNA begins to exit.)

NADYA: Mama wait! Don't go! Listen.

NINA IVANOVNA: What is it, dear?

NADYA: You know how I told you I can't sleep anymore?

NINA IVANOVNA: Yes.

NADYA: Well. . .well, I think I know why. Mama, there's something weighing on my heart. I've been thinking about the things that Sasha tells me. Sasha, this strange, naïve man, he tells me all of his dreams. . .

NINA IVANOVNA: Dreams?

NADYA: Yes, Mama. His dreams of these marvelous fountains and beautiful parks. They're ridiculous. They're *wonderful.* And my heart overflows with joy when he tells me to—

(NADYA stops herself.)

NINA IVANOVNA: To what? What does he tell you to do?

NADYA: Oh Mama, if you only knew what's happening to me! I beg you, I'm pleading with you, let me go away. Please!

NINA IVANOVNA: Where? Where to?

(NADYA can hardly say it.)

NADYA: Let me leave this town! There should not, there *cannot* be any wedding—you have to understand! I don't love this man. . .I can't even talk about him.

NINA IVANOVNA *(frightened)***:** No, my darling, no. Calm down—it's because you're in low spirits. It will pass. This happens. You probably just had a spat with Andrei, but a lovers' tiff always ends in kisses.

NADYA: Oh, go away, Mama, go away.

NINA IVANOVNA: Yes. Not so long ago you were a child, a little girl, and now you're already engaged. But Nature is in a constant state of metabolism. And before you know it, you will be a mother yourself, and then an old woman, and you'll have an obstinate daughter like mine.

NADYA: My dear, my darling, you are intelligent, but you are unhappy. You are very unhappy. You were never happy. You never loved Papa. I see that now! You don't have anything. You depend on grandma.

NINA IVANOVNA: She's like a mother to me.

NADYA: She's your mother-in-law! Dear God! How was it that I thought you were extraordinary? Why haven't I ever seen that you are just an ordinary unhappy woman?

(NINA IVANOVNA starts to leave.)

NADYA: Listen to me! I beg you, think, and try to understand! Just understand how shallow and shameful our life is! My eyes have been opened, I see everything now. And what is Andrei Andreich? He is not intelligent, Mama! Good Lord, my God! Come to your senses, Mama. He's stupid!

NINA IVANOVNA: *Will you stop it!* You and your grandmother. All you do is torture me! Torture! I want to live! *(Beating her fist against her chest.)* To live! Give me my freedom! I'm still young, I want to live, and you have turned me into an old woman!

(NINA IVANOVNA weeps. NADYA goes to SASHA, who is packing.)

NADYA: Sasha. . .Sasha, dear!

SASHA: What is it?

NADYA: How I could have lived here before, I can't understand, I can't comprehend! I despise my fiancé, I despise myself, I despise this entire, idle, meaningless life.

SASHA: There. . .there. It's nothing, everything will be—

NADYA: *No.* Listen to me! This life disgusts me. I can't bear to stay here one more day. I'm leaving. When you leave for Moscow tomorrow, take me with you, for God's sake!

(SASHA looks at her for a moment. He feels her forehead.)

NADYA: Sasha, I'm not sick, I mean it! Take me with you.

SASHA: Oh my goodness. It's wonderful! How *wonderful!* Oh, look at you Nadya! Your eyes! They're so full of life and expectation! Are you sure you're ready!

NADYA: Yes! Yes, Sasha! I'm ready for anything—even *death!*

(He dances around the room.)

SASHA: Tomorrow when I leave, you will come with me to the station to see me off. . .I'll pack your things in my trunk and get your ticket, and when the third bell rings you'll board the train—and we'll be off. You'll go with me as far as Moscow and from there you'll go to Saint Petersburg by yourself. Do you have your passport?

NADYA: Yes.

SASHA: I promise you won't regret this, and you'll never be sorry for it. You'll leave, you'll study, and then let fate carry you wherever it may. The main thing is to turn your life upside-down, nothing else matters. So we leave tomorrow?

NADYA: Oh, yes! For God's sake, yes!

(Thunder and rain. SASHA puts on a long coat, and ENSEMBLE pile luggage into a carriage. MARFA MIKHAILOVNA, NINA IVANOVNA, FATHER ANDREI and ANDREI ANDREICH hold open umbrellas.)

MARFA MIKHAILOVNA: Sasha, you have more luggage than you'll need in a lifetime! Nadya, you won't fit! Why do you want to see him off in such weather? He'll be back next summer. Stay home.

SASHA: Come, Nadya. I don't want to be late.

(SASHA helps her into the carriage.)

MARFA MIKHAILOVNA: Goodbye! God bless! Write when you get to Moscow, Sasha.

SASHA: I will, Granny, I will!

MARFA MIKHAILOVNA: May the Queen of Heaven protect you!

NADYA: Only now did Nadya begin to cry. Only now did she realize that she was really leaving, something she hadn't really believed when she said goodbye to her grandmother, when she had looked at her mother. But all of a sudden she remembered: Andrei and his father, and the new apartment, and the naked lady with the vase, and already none of it seemed frightening or burdensome anymore, but seemed naïve, trivial, and it all retreated further and further away.

(Train whistle.)

SASHA: And when they boarded the train and it began to depart, all of the past, so significant and serious. . .

NADYA: . . .all shrank into a little lump, and a future. . .

SASHA: . . .huge and vast, barely perceptible till now. . .

NADYA: . . .unfolded before her.

SASHA: The rain beat against the windows of the car. . .

NADYA: . . .only green fields were visible now. . .

SASHA: . . .the telegraph poles with birds on the wires flashed by. . .

NADYA: . . .and she remembered that she was traveling toward freedom, toward studying. . .

SASHA: . . .and she laughed and cried and prayed.

NADYA: She was finally free.

(They exit.)

ENSEMBLE: Autumn passed and after it, winter. Nadya was now very homesick and thought every day of her mother and grandma. . .She thought of Sasha too. Letters came from home, quiet and kind, and it seemed that everything had been forgiven and forgotten.

ENSEMBLE *(cont'd)*: She passed her examinations in May. And then she set off, feeling healthy and happy, for home. Stopping along the way in Moscow to see Sasha.
(A Lithography Shop in Moscow. NADYA and SASHA enter.)

SASHA: My God, Nadya has arrived! Welcome to Moscow! My own, dearest one!

NADYA: My dear Sasha! You're just the same as last summer— still the scraggly beard. . .Why don't you ever comb your hair, and get some different clothes! My God, have you lost weight?

(SASHA has a coughing fit. Throughout the following, he tries not to cough.)

NADYA: Sasha. . .Sasha, my God, your cough. . . it's gotten worse.

SASHA: It's nothing, it's nothing. . .

NADYA: Well, no wonder. It's so smoky in here. And those fumes. . .

SASHA: Yes, they're pungent.

NADYA: What are they?

SASHA: India ink, paint. . .

NADYA: Do you live here?

SASHA: Yes. . .I mean, I have a room in the back.

(He laughs, and it becomes a cough.)

NADYA: You still have nothing but contempt for any kind of comfort, don't you?

SASHA: I don't need luxuries.

NADYA: Well your lungs could do without all of these fumes, and dust, and dead flies, and. . . *(Looks at floor.)* Have you been spitting on the floor?

SASHA: Oh. Sometimes, I—

NADYA: Is that blood?

SASHA: And how have you been? *(Pause.)* Nadya?

NADYA: I've been well. Everything has turned out well. In the autumn Mama visited me in Saint Petersburg and told me that Grandmother isn't angry, only that she always walks round my room making the sign of the cross on the walls.

(SASHA laughs and coughs into a handkerchief. The handkerchief comes away bloody.)

NADYA: Sasha. . .dear Sasha, you're sick!

SASHA: I'm sick, but not very.

NADYA: Oh my God. Why haven't you gone to a doctor, why aren't you taking care of yourself? My dear, sweet Sasha. . . you are very, very sick. I would do anything to keep you from being so pale and thin. I owe you so much! You can't imagine how much you have done for me, my dear Sasha! *(Pause.)* Do you know that you are the closest, dearest person in my life?

(Pause.)

SASHA: I'm going to the Volga the day after tomorrow, then I'm drinking *kumis*[5]. I want to try the *kumis* cure. A friend and his wife are going with me. His wife is amazing. I keep pestering her, trying to convince her to go to school. I want her to turn her life upside-down.

NADYA: They sat on talking, but now that Nadya had spent a winter in Saint Petersburg, Sasha—from his words, to his smile, to his whole being—seemed to be outmoded, old-fashioned, something that was finished long ago and, perhaps, had already gone to the grave.

SASHA: On the way to the train station, Sasha treated her to tea and apples.

---

[5] Fermented mare's milk.

NADYA: And as the train departed and he waved his handkerchief with a smile, it was apparent just by looking at his legs that he was very ill and didn't have long to live.

(NINA IVANOVNA and MARFA MIKHAILOVNA appear.)

NADYA: It was noon when she arrived at her town.

NINA IVANOVNA: My darling! My own darling!

MARFA MIKHAILOVNA: My own! My baby!

NADYA: Grandma looked as old, and as stout and plain as ever. Mama had aged too, and seemed to have shrunk, but she still wore her corset too tight and diamonds sparkled on every finger.

(MARFA MIKHAILOVNA goes out.)

NINA IVANOVNA: Well, Nadya, how is everything? Are you content, really content?

NADYA: Yes, I'm content.

NINA IVANOVNA: I've become religious. You know, I'm studying philosophy now, and I'm thinking, always thinking. . . And now I see everything as clear as day. First of all, it seems to me, that it's necessary for all of life to pass as through a prism.

NADYA: Tell me, Mama, how is Grandmother's health?

NINA IVANOVNA: She's doing fine. When you left with Sasha and we received your telegram, she collapsed as she read it. She didn't move for three days. After that, she just kept praying to God and crying, but now she's fine.

(NINA IVANOVNA begins to fade away.)

NINA IVANOVNA: Anyway, as I was saying, our entire life must pass as if through a prism. In other words, our consciousness must be divided into its simplest elements, like the seven primary colors, and each element must be studied separately. . .

(NINA IVANOVNA has disappeared. NADYA is alone.)

NADYA: May passed and June came. Already, Nadya had grown used to being home. Grandmother fussed over the samovar. Nina Ivanovna still lived in the house like a beggar and in the evenings talked philosophy. Nadya would stroll through the streets, looking at the houses and the gray fences, and it seemed to her that everything in the town had long ago grown old, had worn out, and all of it was just waiting either for the end, or maybe for the beginning of something young and fresh. Oh, that this new, clear life would arrive soon! A time will come when not one trace of Grandmother's house, in which four servants had to live in one room in a filthy basement, will be left. It will be forgotten, and nobody will be left to remember it.

(NINA IVANOVNA appears.)

NINA IVANOVNA: A letter came from Sarátov. *(Hands a letter to NADYA.)*

NADYA: From Sasha!

(SASHA appears.)

NADYA: It was in his happy, dancing handwriting. . .

SASHA & NADYA: . . .that the trip down the Volga had been a complete success. . .

SASHA: . . .except that I became sick in Sarátov and had to spend two weeks in the hospital.

(He goes.)

ENSEMBLE: Nadya had an overwhelming premonition. But she was troubled that it did not bother her as it once had. She wanted to return to Saint Petersburg, and her friendship with Sasha, though something she treasured, already seemed to be in the distant, distant past! She did not sleep all night and sat at the window. When she went downstairs in the morning, Granny was standing in the corner of the room praying, and her face was stained with tears. On the table lay a telegram.

(ENSEMBLE hands NADYA a telegram.)

NADYA *(reading)*: "Yesterday morning, in Sarátov, Alexander Timoféich, Sasha for short, died of consumption."

(FATHER ANDREI appears and chants the Russian Orthodox rites of the dead. NINA IVANOVNA and MARFA MIKHAILOVNA enter. They both kneel as FATHER ANDREI continues to chant.)

NINA IVANOVNA: Granny and Nina Ivanovna went to the church to arrange a funeral mass.

NADYA: Nadya walked around the rooms for a long time, thinking. She realized clearly that her life had been turned upside-down, just as Sasha had wanted, and that her past had been torn away and burned, and the ashes scattered to the wind.

ENSEMBLE: She went into Sasha's room and stood there.

NADYA: She envisioned a new, wide, spacious life ahead, and that life, still obscure and full of mysteries, enticed and called to her.

ENSEMBLE: She went to her room upstairs to pack, and the next day she said goodbye to her family.

(FATHER ANDREI stops chanting.)

NINA IVANOVNA: And happy. . .

MARFA MIKHAILOVNA: . . .and full of life. . .

NADYA: . . .she left the town—as she believed—forever.

END OF PLAY

James Serpento

The Doctor

a play

inspired by the stories
"The Doctor" and "A Work of Art"

from translations by R. Andrew White
with Jane Martsinovsky Hendricks

The Doctor was first presented by Mad Genie Productions, Chicago, IL in March, 1994. It was directed by Christine Hartman, with the following cast:

NIKOLAI	R. Andrew White
OLGA	Tricia Kym Armstrong
MISHA	Grady Hutt
SHASHKIN	David Mitchell Ghilardi

CHARACTERS

NIKOLÁI, a doctor

ÓLGA, a mother

MÍSHA, a boy of nine

SHÁSHKIN, a comic

SETTING

A drawing room and child's bedroom in Olga's house; and the dressing room of a theatre.

James Serpento

The Doctor

a play

inspired by the stories
"The Doctor" and "A Work of Art,"

by Anton Chekhov

from translations by
R. Andrew White

with Jane Martsinovsky Hendricks

I

(*Lights up on a drawing room. OLGA stands, looking front, as looking out a window. NIKOLAI sits in a chair. He quietly tosses his hat into the air and catches it on his finger; he does this twice, but on the third time, he misses and the hat falls onto the floor. As he stoops to pick it up:*)

NIKOLAI: (Oopsy.)

OLGA: Ssh...

(*NIKOLAI stops, mid-stoop.*)

NIKOLAI: Hm?

OLGA: Ssh...Listen. (*Pause*) Listen.

(*Silence. NIKOLAI remains frozen in mid-stoop.*)

NIKOLAI: Do you hear a burglar?

OLGA: No. A fly. Do you hear it? (*Silence.*) Zzt. Zzt. He sounds like he's. . .on the ceiling. (*Looks up.*) Yes. There. See?

NIKOLAI (*looks up*): Yep. There he is.

OLGA (*still looking up*): There is nothing more unimaginably horrible.

NIKOLAI: Oh, I don't know. He's not very big.

(*OLGA looks at NIKOLAI in silence. Then:*)

OLGA: Are you joking with me?

(*Silence.*)

NIKOLAI: No. No. I'm sorry.

(*OLGA turns again and looks out the window.*)

OLGA: Zzt. Zzt. Zzt. (*Pause.*) He's moved to. . .the draperies. Yes? (*Looks to her right.*) Yes. There he is. My senses are. . . I don't know. My senses are improving. Like. . . it's like I'm drawing his. . . his life into me, the things he. . .

NIKOLAI: . . .oh, now. . .

OLGA: . . .the things he won't need anymore.

(*NIKOLAI moves to OLGA, touches her shoulders lightly. She stiffens a little.*)

OLGA: I can't survive it.

NIKOLAI: . . .now. . .

OLGA: I can't. He is my joy, my happiness, my wealth. If I cease to be his—

NIKOLAI: You can never cease that, no matter what happens—

OLGA: —I will be a shadow. I will be a ghost.

(*Silence. NIKOLAI returns to his chair and sits.*)

(*OLGA crosses, as to another window.*)

OLGA: I was vulgar. Stupid. (*Beat*) *Feather*headed.

NIKOLAI: That was a long time ago.

OLGA: Yes. (*Pause.*) The lake looks. . .deep. Deeper today. Is that possible?

NIKOLAI: I don't think so. I think the depth of a lake is a fairly. . . fixed. . .thing. Unless you figure your normal patterns of evolution, which are, of course, heavily impacted by things like. . . time. Fish. Marine. . .things. I think it's a fairly. . .fixed thing.

OLGA: Mm.

(*Silence.*)

OLGA: You are a frivolous man, Nicky. Do you know that?

NIKOLAI: Mm-hm.

OLGA: Frivolous. You belong in the zoo—

NIKOLAI (*overlapping at "zoo"*): Circus, yes—

OLGA: —no, the *zoo*.

(*Silence.*)

OLGA: Frivolous, but I do not give up hope.

NIKOLAI: You know, you're right. You're *right*, by. . . gosh, but. . . frivolous, *yes*, but. . .I know a fact when I see one, if only so that I know to go whistling by it. (*Laughs weakly. Pause.*) I know the *facts*, Olga. And there is a hideous one (if I may, bear *with* me, please) there is a hideous fact which we must face.

OLGA: You're a doctor.

NIKOLAI: Which qualifies me to answer questions, yes—

OLGA: You're becoming frantic again, Nicky.

NIKOLAI: —I mean, I can answer as many questions as you like, but that only *illuminates* the fact, it doesn't *change* it. Eh? You see?

(*OLGA weeps. NIKOLAI walks, twirling his hat between his hands.*)

NIKOLAI: I'm not *God*, I'm not even. . .mm. (*Pause.*) Well. I'm not all those wonderful "things." No. That one reads about in storybooks, *no*. About doctors or. . .knights in shining. . .mm. So: If you'll spare me a moment's attention. If you'll do that, there is something of tremendous importance that I must ask you. Incalculable importance.

(*Silence, as OLGA turns to face NIKOLAI.*)

NIKOLAI: Oh. Perhaps after lunch.

*

II

(*A bedroom in the house. A boy of nine, MISHA, is in his sickbed, lying on his back, staring straight up, unblinking. NIKOLAI approaches.*)

NIKOLAI: Misha?

(*Silence. NIKOLAI lowers his head.*)

NIKOLAI: Misha. . .

(*Silence.*)

MISHA: There are flies in here.

NIKOLAI: Oh! Oh, yes, there certainly are. Your mother was listening to them before, following them with her ears.

MISHA: Do they think I'm dead?

(*Silence.*)

NIKOLAI: Well. . .I don't know.

MISHA: I haven't moved for a while.

MISHA *(cont'd)*: They must think I'm dead.

NIKOLAI: Perhaps. They're not too bright, flies. I mean, how could they be? They can't have much for brains, look at them, where would they *put* one? Enough to do just with wings and more legs than they need, so forth. (*Pause. Sighs.*) Does your head ache?

MISHA: Yes. So what?

NIKOLAI: Well, I'm your doctor, it's a fairly routine question given your condition, I—

MISHA: I keep dreaming.

(*Silence.*)

NIKOLAI: Oh. What do you dream?

MISHA: All sorts of things.

(*Silence.*)

NIKOLAI: Would you like to talk about them?

MISHA: No. (*Pause.*) What for?

NIKOLAI: It might. . .put you at ease, might, you know, take your mind off your—

MISHA: Imminent death?

NIKOLAI: Where did you learn a word like that?

(*Silence.*)

MISHA: "Death?"

NIKOLAI: "Imminent."

MISHA: I dreamed it. Is it a real word?

NIKOLAI: Oh, yes. Oh! I know! You probably heard me use that phrase while you were asleep, but you weren't truly asleep, you could still sort of hear things in your sleep, and I said that—

MISHA: Then I *am* dying.

NIKOLAI: —you—you. . . (*Pause.*) I'm sorry. (*Pause.*) I'm sorry, what did you say?

(*Silence.*)

MISHA: That I dream.

NIKOLAI: Ah. True enough.

MISHA: I dream about girls.

NIKOLAI: Oh! Well. Well, that just means that you must be feeling better. (*Chuckles.*) Feeling *healthier.* Any particular girl you dream of?

MISHA: Two girls.

NIKOLAI: Ah. Doubly healthy, then, eh? (*Chuckles.*)

MISHA: Two girls. (*Pause.*) Doing things. (*Pause.*) Together.

NIKOLAI: Two girls. Doing things. Together. (*Pause.*) Ahhhhmmm. Sewing? (*Pause.*) Cooking? (*Pause.*) Perhaps a game of croquet?

MISHA: Look under my bed.

(*Silence.*)

NIKOLAI: Whatever for?

MISHA: You won't know till you've done it, will you?

(*Silence. NIKOLAI gets to his knees and looks under MISHA's bed.*)

NIKOLAI: Well. . .

MISHA: Do you see it?

NIKOLAI: (. . .awful lot of dust, that's what I—)

MISHA: There should be a box.

(*NIKOLAI stands, having pulled a box out from under the bed.*)

NIKOLAI: Yes. Yes. Here it is. (You could have asked the maid to do that. . .)

MISHA: (*Laughing a little.*) Oh, I don't think so. . .

NIKOLAI: (*Overlapping.*) Brand new pants, look at that.

MISHA: Why don't you look inside.

NIKOLAI: There aren't any of those. . .*things*, you know, that *spring* out at you. Are there? Because I'm very tired.

MISHA: Nothing like that.

(*Pause. NIKOLAI looks inside the box. Silence.*)

MISHA: It's a book end. It's one book end. If I had the other in the set, there'd be four. . .

NIKOLAI: . . .four. . .

MISHA: . . .four girls altogether. (*Pause.*) Doing things. (*Pause.*) But I've only got the one. So there's only two. . .

NIKOLAI: (*Turning his head as he looks into the box.*) . . . two, yes, I see. . .

MISHA: . . .two girls. . .

NIKOLAI: . . . doing things. Aaaaahhhhmmmm. (*Pause.*) Who made this?

MISHA: I don't know.

NIKOLAI: (*Absently, as he peeks into the box.*) Have to be a specialist of one kind or another, I imagine.

MISHA: It was in a shop. Mama took me to the bazaar and I let go of her hand and slipped through the crowd like a ghost. Nobody could see me. I went into a shop. And there it was. One bookend. Two girls. Doing things. It was under a sign. The sign said "Erotica." (*Pause.*) "E-ro-ti-ca." (*Pause.*) What's "Erotica?"

NIKOLAI: (*Absently, as he peeks into the box again.*) Two girls doing things, I imagine. (*Closes the box firmly.*) The shopkeeper sold you this?

MISHA: Yes. He smiled and said it was nice. He said it was a real work of art.

NIKOLAI: Work of art, eh? Common criminal, selling this to a child.

MISHA: I'm an adult. My lifetime's almost over. I'm an old man for my years.

NIKOLAI: (*Pause.*) Does your mother know you have this?

(*Silence. MISHA smiles.*)

MISHA: I gave the shopkeeper all my money. It wasn't much because it was only the one. Now, if it had been *both*. . .

NIKOLAI: (*Overlapping.*) . . .both bookends, all four girls, yes. . .

MISHA: . . .that would have cost a pretty penny, I'll bet. Almost as much as *real* girls—

NIKOLAI: Ssh—!

MISHA: —doing things—

NIKOLAI: See here—!

(*MISHA giggles.*)

NIKOLAI: —your mother is in the next room—!

MISHA: (*Whispers.*) —all *right*, she doesn't know. (*Pause.*) She has no idea I have it. (*Pause.*) All right? (*Pause.*) I walked all the way home, one hand in hers, the other hand here— (*puts his hand on his lower belly*) — holding the box under my big coat.

(*Silence.*)

MISHA: Sometimes I imagine it's mother. One of the two girls. . .

NIKOLAI: You're feverish—

MISHA: What? She's a grown-up, just like me—

NIKOLAI: —you must be feverish, you must be—

MISHA: I'm fine.

NIKOLAI: Well, you are. I mean, you're fev— never mi— God.

(*NIKOLAI touches MISHA's forehead.*)

NIKOLAI: And you are *not* fine. As I thought, you are fev—

MISHA: I don't feel a thing.

NIKOLAI: Well, of course, because—because you are—*upset*, you are—

MISHA: I'm not upset—

NIKOLAI: (*Tense whisper.*) It's the only thing! It's the only—acceptable explanation for, for, for—your *obscenities*. The only thing!

(*Silence.*)

MISHA: Do you think mother would like it?

NIKOLAI: (*Absently.*) I'm sure I have no idea—No! No, of course not! I mean, how would I know a thing like that, or why are you even *thinking* about it, here you are on your *death*bed, you—

(*Silence.*)

NIKOLAI: Your. . .sickbed, now *see*? You shouldn't be getting yourself all upset.

MISHA: I'm not upset.

(*Silence.*)

NIKOLAI: Oh. Well, that's. . .I mean, that's not *normal*.

(*Silence.*)

MISHA: Sometimes I feel a little. . .e-ro-ti-ca.

NIKOLAI: (*Absently.*) "Erotic."

Misha: Oh.

Nikolai: I *think*, I mean I don't *know*—

(*Misha giggles.*)

Nikolai: Stop that! (*Pause. Starts to put the box away.*) Well, I'll just—

Misha: No.

Nikolai: No?

Misha: No. (*Pause.*) I want you to have it. It's my gift to you. You did everything you could for me and so I want you to have it.

Nikolai: I, I, I, I, I, I couldn't possibly—

Misha: Sssh. (*Pause.*) It's a work of art. (*Pause.*) To remember me by. (*Pause.*) It's my dying wish.

*

III

(*The drawing room. Olga sits, staring. There is a noise, off.*)

Olga: Nicky?

Nikolai: (*Off.*) I'm just going. . .

Olga: What?

Nikolai: (*Off.*) . . .I'll let myself out, don't bother—

Olga: *What?* Come in here! (*As she paces.*) You need to tell me what his *progress* is, for heaven's sake, do I increase the *dosage*, what do I *do* with him?

(*Nikolai enters. He holds his hat over his lower belly. Olga doesn't immediately see him.*)

Olga: Nikolai—? (*Turns and sees Nikolai.*) Oh. There you are. Well, what's the report?

NIKOLAI: He's. . .pretty much the same.

(*OLGA sits, and begins to weep.*)

NIKOLAI: (*Pause.*) One or two particulars, nothing to worry about. Pretty much the same.

(*OLGA weeps harder.*)

NIKOLAI: What can I say? What is it *possible* to say?

(*OLGA's weeping intensifies. NIKOLAI goes to her. With one hand he pats her shoulder; with the other, he holds his hat over his lower belly.*)

OLGA: Hold me.

(*NIKOLAI doesn't move.*)

OLGA: Please hold me. Please.

(*NIKOLAI keeps one hand on his hat, which he continues to hold over his belly. He does his best to put his other arm strongly around OLGA's shoulders. OLGA weeps harder.*)

OLGA: You hate me.

NIKOLAI: No—

OLGA: I'm a *pariah* to you—

NIKOLAI: No—

OLGA: —a sick joke you want to forget you told.

NIKOLAI: No—

OLGA: You do, you do, you *hate* me and I don't under*stand*—

NIKOLAI: Well—

OLGA: You're *cold* to me. Now, when I need you the most, you're *cold*—

NIKOLAI: I don't know what to say to you—

OLGA: My little boy is *dying,* you could at least not rush out of the *house* like it's on *fire,* you could at least PUT DOWN YOUR GODDAMNED HAT!

(*Silence. NIKOLAI puts down his hat, revealing a large bulge at his belly, under his sweater. Silence.*)

OLGA: What's wrong with your stomach?

NIKOLAI: Oh. Well. . .My what?

OLGA: Your *stomach.*

(*Silence.*)

NIKOLAI: It's my lunch.

OLGA (*giggles a little*)**:** Did you eat a rock?

NIKOLAI (*laughing*)**:** No, no. Cook made me a lunch, put it in a box, I was, I thought I was *leaving,* you understand, I didn't want it to get wet.

(*They both look front, as out the window.*)

NIKOLAI: Well, in case it. . . (*Silence.*) So I. . .you know:

(*He makes a gesture of jamming something into his sweater.*)

OLGA: What did she make you?

NIKOLAI: A thing. Just a little thing. Little pastry thing. How are you feeling, better?

OLGA: I feel. . .I feel. . .You look absurd.

NIKOLAI: Oh! Oh, yes, I suppose I do. Well, if you're feeling better—

OLGA: Stay with me tonight—

NIKOLAI: —I couldn't. I couldn't do that. . .

OLGA (*overlapping*)**:** . . .why not? I'm not— I'm not seducing you, Nicky. . .

NIKOLAI (*overlapping*): . . .it's not proper, it's not—*you* know better than that. . .

OLGA (*overlapping*): . . .what if he—what if he needs something? You're miles away. What if he, Nicky, *what if he dies in the night?!* (*Silence.*) What if he dies? (*Silence.*) Please.

(*Silence.*)

NIKOLAI: I have other patients.

(*Silence.*)

OLGA: You. . .*filth.*

NIKOLAI: I have asked you repeatedly, I have—you—if—*if* you have something to say to me about that boy, something to tell me about just what his relationship is to me—*if*—I have told you to tell me and you lie. You *lie.* You don't know, you say.

(*OLGA begins to giggle.*)

NIKOLAI: There are two, not *one*, mind you, but *two* other men who could make the claims I might make in this situation. What do you say to them? Eh? *Eh?* What do you THINK YOU ARE LAUGHING AT?

OLGA: I'm sorry. I'm sorry. It's just. . .you look like a circus clown. You do. Put the lunch on the table. Put it on the table.

(*Beat. NIKOLAI removes the box from under his sweater and places it on the table.*)

OLGA: Now, we can discuss this like adults. (*Pause. Reaches for the box.*) Shall we share lunch? You must be famished.

NIKOLAI: (*Grabs the box back.*) Well, you'll have to get your own lunch then. This is mine.

(*Silence.*)

OLGA: What a strange time for you to make claims to ownership.

*

IV

(*Backstage at a theatre. NIKOLAI sits on a chair, the box in his lap. Sound of a fly buzzing nearby. Sound of laughter offstage, followed by more laughter, then more laughter, then applause, then music. Pause. SHASHKIN enters, in a clown-tramp costume, with false red nose. Pause, as the two men look at each other.*)

SHASHKIN: Nikolai?

NIKOLAI: Hello again, Shashkin—

SHASHKIN: *Nikolai?*

NIKOLAI: Hello again—

(*SHASHKIN rushes to NIKOLAI and shakes his hand vigorously.*)

SHASHKIN: Old Nicky. My *God.* Yes? Ha! Full of the old nick, was old Nicky. It's a great pleasure to see you, my friend, how in the hell did you get in here?

NIKOLAI: A man out back—

SHASHKIN: —by the stage door—?

NIKOLAI: —he let me in.

SHASHKIN: Well, he's not supposed to do that. (*Pause.*) But I'm certainly glad he did this time, eh? (*Laughs, and punches Nikolai in the shoulder. Pause.*) Sit down, why don't you.

(*NIKOLAI doesn't sit. SHASHKIN sits at his dressing table and begins to remove his stage make-up.*)

SHASHKIN: Did you bring me a present?

NIKOLAI: Oh! Oh, yes, as a matter of fact, I did.

NIKOLAI *(cont'd):* Testament to all the years gone by and all that. It's for you.

(*NIKOLAI puts the box on the dressing table, starts to leave.*)

NIKOLAI: Well, it's been a great pleasure seeing you again, please take care of yourself, I know you'll be a great star one day.

(*SHASHKIN has looked inside the box.*)

SHASHKIN: Wait. (*Pause.*) What is this about?

NIKOLAI: Hm? (*Pause.*) It's a work of art.

(*SHASHKIN looks inside the box again.*)

NIKOLAI: It's a bookend.

SHASHKIN: Only one.

NIKOLAI: Correct.

SHASHKIN: There are two, uh. . . (*Pause.*)

NIKOLAI: Also correct! But they're. . .connected. See? It's just one bookend, but two girls, all. . . connected there. . .listen, it's still good, who needs another one? You just get *creative*—

SHASHKIN: What am I to do with this?

NIKOLAI: (*Beat.*) You get creative. (*Pause.*) It's a work of art, you see. You being an artist, you know, I thought—

SHASHKIN: Uh-huh.

NIKOLAI: (*Pause.*) You being an artist. Of sorts.

SHASHKIN: I tell jokes and walk funny. That doesn't make me an artist, Nicky, and it doesn't make me a pornographer either.

NIKOLAI: No no no no no no no no no. This, my dear fellow, is *erotica*. I just meant that you have an eye for the finer things that I don't possess. So I thought you'd like this.

SHASHKIN: Just what is this about? (*Pause.*) Is this blackmail?

NIKOLAI: No no no no no no no no no.

SHASHKIN: You said that already.

NIKOLAI: It's a work of art. Erotica. (*Pause.*) Please,
Shashkin. Please take it. It was given to me by a patient, but
I can't have that in my house. I'm a respected person.

(*SHASHKIN nods, smiles, looks away.*)

NIKOLAI: What am I to do? All I can do is pass along the
gift, knowing that it's going to someone who appreciates it.
As *I* do, but I can't have it.

SHASHKIN: Put it in a closet, why don't you?

NIKOLAI: It came from a patient, Shashkin. His dying wish
was that I have it. I can't just put it in a closet.

SHASHKIN: But you can give it away.

NIKOLAI: To someone who *appreciates* it. As I do. But I can't
accept it.

SHASHKIN: Who's the patient?

NIKOLAI: A. . .a boy.

(*Silence.*)

NIKOLAI: Olga's little boy.

SHASHKIN: Olga?

NIKOLAI: Olga.

(*Silence.*)

SHASHKIN: So many years ago. Olga. Old. . .Gah. (*Expels
breath in a sensuous sigh.*) Gaaaahhhh. (*Pause.*) There
were several people in that room so many years ago, Nicky.
Several bottles, several laughing voices, several sighs.
Several pleasures taken. Several, but certain, pleasures—I
may say—*liberties*, taken. (*Pause.*) What are you up to?

NIKOLAI: Nothing, I'm just giving you—

SHASHKIN: To me. (*Pause.*) Give it to Vladimir, why don't you? (*Pause.*) Hm? (*Pause.*) It's his as much as ours. Isn't it? (*Shrugs. Pause.*)

NIKOLAI: Vladimir is dead. Suicide. They say.

(*Beat. SHASHKIN smiles a little, snorts.*)

SHASHKIN: Well.

(*SHASHKIN makes a quick sign of the cross on himself, knocks three times on his dressing table, turns his head to the left and spits three times.*)

SHASHKIN: He was always a bunny rabbit anyway. (*Pause.*) Did she put you up to this?

NIKOLAI: She doesn't know I have it! Doesn't know a thing about it! Nothing! What do you think it would do to her to find out her little boy, her *dying child* for God's sake, has a thing like that under his bed! A piece of "erotica"! It would *destroy* her, that's what! (*Pause.*) The thoughts he has, you have to understand! I fear for his soul!

(*Silence.*)

NIKOLAI: But he gives me this and—do you see?—maybe *giving* something, giving a *gift,* maybe that's to be his redemption. (*Pause.*) Eh? (*Pause.*) *It's our fault, Shashkin!* (*Pause.*) I know we've had words in the past.

SHASHKIN: More than words, old Nick. We've shared more than words. Haven't we. (*Pause.*) He's not mine, old boy.

NIKOLAI: How do you know?

SHASHKIN: I decided he's not. (*Pause. A terrible roar:*) I DECIDED HE'S NOT!

(*Silence. The two men look at each other.*)

SHASHKIN: But I'll take it. For old time's sake. (*Pause.*) How'll that be?

*

V

(*The drawing room. OLGA stands as before. NIKOLAI is again in the chair, tossing his hat. He catches it on his finger, once, twice, thrice.*)

NIKOLAI (*of catching the hat*): Well!

(*There comes a slight hitch in OLGA's breath.*)

NIKOLAI: I know there's not much consolation. Is there.

OLGA: No.

NIKOLAI: He was a good boy.

(*OLGA sighs deeply.*)

NIKOLAI: He was *good*. (*Pause.*) He was *good*. You must know that.

OLGA: Yes. . .

NIKOLAI: . . .a good, good boy. . .

OLGA (*as she weeps*): . . .yes. . .

NIKOLAI: . . .delightful. . .

OLGA: . . .yes. . .

NIKOLAI: . . .delightful sense of humor. . .

OLGA: . . .yes he did. . .

NIKOLAI: . . .wise beyond his years. . .

OLGA: . . .yes. . .

NIKOLAI: . . .a *good* boy.

(*OLGA's weeping subsides into silence.*)

OLGA: How long now?

NIKOLAI: Hm? Oh. (*Pause, as he looks at his watch.*) Since they took him away, about. . .four and a half hours.

OLGA: I can't bear it.

NIKOLAI: Sssh. . .

OLGA: I'll never be able to live another day, I'll never make it—

NIKOLAI: . . .sssh. . .

OLGA: *—it's only been four and a half hours??!!*

(*Silence.*)

NIKOLAI: Well, it's actually been more than eight since he died. (*Pause.*) See? (*Pause.*) Things are never as bad as they seem.

(*Silence. OLGA slaps NIKOLAI across the face. A bell rings offstage.*)

NIKOLAI: Do you want me to—?

OLGA: No. I'm the lady of the house. You're just the doctor.

(*OLGA exits. NIKOLAI tosses his hat into the air.*)

NIKOLAI: Ah! There's that fly, I see him. Right there. Let me see. (*Closes his eyes.*) Zzzt. Zzzt. Zzzzzzt.

(*OLGA returns and stands in the doorway, holding the box, now wrapped in brown paper.*)

NIKOLAI: Let's see. He's riiiiiight. . .there.

(*NIKOLAI turns and points, opening his eyes. He's pointing at OLGA, as she stands, holding the box.*)

OLGA: This was just delivered.

NIKOLAI: Oh?

OLGA: It says it's from Shashkin.

(*Silence.*)

NIKOLAI: Really.

OLGA: It's addressed to both of us.

NIKOLAI: You don't say.

OLGA: Why would Shashkin be contacting us?

(*Silence.*)

NIKOLAI: He's a comedian on the stage now. Did you know that? (*Pause.*) Hm. (*Pause.)* That fly. That fly came back. I'll bet it's the same damned one. See him up there? See him? (*Pause.*) Zzzt. Zzzt. (*Pause.*) Sssh. Listen. . .listen. (*Pause.*) It came back.

END OF PLAY

R. Andrew White

Zina

a play

suggested by the short story
"A Story Without an End" by Anton Chekhov

translated by R. Andrew White
with Jane Martsinovky Hendricks

An earlier version of this play was presented by Mad Genie Productions, Chicago, IL in March, 1994. It was directed by Christine Hartman. The cast was as follows:

MAN   David Mitchell Ghilardi

PETER   R. Andrew White

CHARACTERS

A MAN

PETER

SETTING

The stage, empty, representing a downstairs room.

R. Andrew White

Zina

a play

suggested by the short story
"A Story without an End" by Anton Chekhov

translated by R. Andrew White
with Jane Martsinovsky Hendricks

(A wooden chair on an empty stage. Several moments of silence. A gunshot.

A MAN, holding a smoking revolver, stumbles in. He wears a white shirt, the lower left side of which is soaked in fresh blood. He staggers for a moment and falls flat to the floor. He lies there for several moments, breathing heavily. Then the breathing ceases.

A long silence.

From behind the draperies comes the sudden, rapid sound of footsteps rushing down a flight of wooden steps.

A second man, PETER, carrying a hoe, enters through the draperies. He pauses for a moment, a little winded. He then drops the hoe and quickly moves to the MAN.

He examines the body, placing a finger on the first MAN's neck. PETER quickly gets up and starts to exit.)

MAN: Zina?

PETER: No.

MAN: Are you an angel?

PETER: I'm Peter.

MAN *(pause)***:** Then you must be a saint, eh?

PETER: I'm your *neighbor.*

MAN: I do not quite. . .*recollect* you at this moment.

PETER: There is no reason you should.

MAN: Well (Peter is it?) welcome to my basement.

PETER: Thank you. Listen, I am—

MAN: Please. Sit down. So I can see you.

PETER: I think it's a doctor you need to see. Now.

MAN: Don't.

PETER: I'm going to get a doc—

MAN: Don't.

PETER: Listen.

MAN *(puts the gun to his head)***:** If you leave, then I will be dead when you return.

(PETER freezes. Silence.)

MAN: You would not want that on your hands, would you?

PETER: *(considers for a moment)* No. No, I wouldn't.

MAN: So, please. Pull up a chair.

(PETER takes the chair and moves it a little closer to the MAN. Sits. Silence.)

PETER: I do not want you to die.

MAN: I want my wife back.

PETER: Zina is *dead*. You cannot *have* her back.

MAN: How do *you* know she's dead?

PETER: I knew her. We would see each other in our gardens. We would talk over the fence. *(Pause.)* I saw her buried.

MAN: She resembled a ghost when they put her in the ground. So *pallid* was her. . .her. . .

PETER: . . .countenance. . .

MAN: . . .yes. . .

PETER: She was pale in life. A pale, beautiful. . .

MAN: . . .ghost.

PETER: *(After a beat.)* Give me the gun. Let me get a doctor, my friend. Allow me. . .

MAN: (Peter. . .)

PETER: . . .to save you.

MAN: What led you here? To my basement?

PETER: I was out in the garden, you see?

MAN: *Garden.*

PETER: Tending the flowers.

MAN: Zina *loved* flowers.

PETER: White chrysanthemums.

MAN *(smiling)*: Yes, yes.

PETER: They were her favorite.

MAN *(still smiling)*: "Mums."

PETER: And I heard your gun.

MAN: She was my flower.

PETER: I had to break your door in.

MAN: My flower.

PETER: With my hoe.

MAN: You are a *good* neighbor, eh?

PETER: Not if I let you die. . .

(The MAN gasps and his body jerks. PETER starts to move toward him, but the MAN quickly re-adjusts the revolver to his head. PETER stops.)

PETER: That would be the same. . .

MAN: . . .Peter. . .

PETER: . . .as if I pulled the trigger. What?

MAN: Do you know why I'm doing this?

PETER: Zina.

MAN: "Unrequited Love," then? Is that how it appears?

PETER: No, it is only Love. *(Pause.)* Or fear perhaps.

MAN: *Fear.* Yes.

PETER: Of life without her.

MAN: Of death without her. *(Pause.)* Love and fear. Ah, well, that's what they write songs about, eh?

(MAN gasps again and his body jerks. He drops the revolver and PETER rushes to him. PETER turns him so that he is lying on his back in PETER'S lap.)

MAN: You know. . .you know, it's funny. No one understands the psychological subtleties of suicide. . .

PETER: *What?*

MAN: . . .oh, I'm not going to lecture, I just think it's funny. Funny thought at the moment of truth, eh? No, God alone understands the *soul* of a man when he takes his own life. Men? No. They don't—

(The MAN gasps and jerks again, clutching his side.)

MAN: I think maybe. . .

PETER: . . .ssh. . .

MAN: . . .I should have shot myself in the temple. . .

PETER: . . .no. . .

MAN: . . .the mouth perhaps. . .

PETER: . . .ssh. . .

MAN: . . .I mean, Peter, this *hurts*. . .

PETER *(holding him close):* . . .just have your own terrible moment. Just have your own terrible moment.

(Silence. PETER looks closely at the MAN.)

PETER: Your earlobes are curling under. . .

(Pause, as PETER and the MAN seem to relax together.)

MAN: Peter?

PETER: Yes?

MAN: I hope you won't think. . .

PETER: . . .ssh. . .

MAN: . . .I'm putting you on the *spot*. . .

PETER: . . .ssh—

MAN: I want to *thank* you, Peter. *(Pause.)* There was a man. . .an—another man.

PETER: Yes?

MAN: Took my Zina away from me.

PETER: *(Pause.)* Did she love him?

MAN: More than the world, she told me, in her little-girl child-like way.

PETER: That much.

MAN: And although she would never say his name, she. . . she. . .

PETER: . . .gave herself to him.

MAN: But I knew she still loved *me. (Pause.)* I told her it would pass. *(Pause.)* For she was so young. So *innocent.*

PETER: A child.

MAN: I wanted to *protect* her.

PETER: Yes.

MAN: So when I put the poison in her tea. . .

PETER: . . .poison. . .

MAN: . . .I knew, you see, that I would take her *back.*

PETER: In her *tea.*

MAN: So thank you, my friend.

PETER: Oh, my. . .

MAN: I took her back.

PETER:. . .*Christ.*

(Silence.)

MAN: So finish me, Peter. *(Pause.)* I long to be in her arms.

PETER: Zina.

MAN: We will be with you always.

PETER: No.

MAN: In your *heart*, Peter.

PETER: (Oh, my God.)

MAN: Until the day of your death. *(Silence.)* So kill me, Peter, and we will be with you. *(Pause.) With* you. *(Pause.)* Ten years. *(Pause.)* Twenty. *(Pause.)* One hundred. *(Pause.)* Until you die. *(Pause.)* Zina and I.

(Silence. PETER gently places the MAN on the ground and gets to his feet in a daze. The MAN gasps again and PETER picks up the revolver and aims it at the MAN; hold. PETER pulls the trigger: click. He pulls again. Click. Again: click. He pulls again and again: Click click click click click click. Lights click to black.)

END OF PLAY

James Serpento

The Ninny

Four Scenes from a Romance

inspired by the short story
by Anton Chekhov

translated by R. Andrew White

The Ninny was first presented by the Repertory Theater of Iowa in Des Moines. It was directed by Richard Maynard and James Serpento, and designed by Jay Michael Jagim. The cast was as follows:

ARLENE	Kim Grimaldi
JULIA	Shoshana Salowitz

CHARACTERS

ARLENE, an actress of fifty

JULIA, an actress of twenty

SETTING

A stage, at night, after a performance of a Chekhovian play.

James Serpento

The Ninny
Four Scenes from a Romance

inspired by the story by Anton Chekhov

as translated by R. Andrew White

I

As Long As We've Bumped Into Each Other

(A stage, after a performance. Not much light. Footsteps. Then, out of the surrounding darkness steps ARLENE, a woman of fifty. She sits on a nearby stool and looks around. The space is deeply silent. Then, somewhere, a heavy door closes. ARLENE starts.)

ARLENE *(looks around, then speaks into the dark)*: Yes? *(Pause.)* Yes?

(There is a crash offstage, behind ARLENE, followed by another woman's voice:)

UNSEEN WOMAN (JULIA): *Oh. Ow.*

ARLENE *(into the dark)*: Yes?

JULIA: Oh, oh, oh. *Shoot.*

ARLENE: Yes?

(Long silence. ARLENE stands, peers into the dark.)

ARLENE *(a joke)*: Friend or foe?

(Silence. Then JULIA enters, a young woman of barely twenty years. She half-walks, half-hops, into the space.)

JULIA: Sorry. Sorry.

ARLENE: Oh, my God. . .

JULIA: I'm so sorry. . .

ARLENE: What the hell did you do?

JULIA: (Such a klutz. . .)

ARLENE: All right, all right, sit.

(ARLENE helps JULIA onto the stool.)

JULIA: There's that, that *thing*, backstage.

ARLENE: Oh, yes.

JULIA: I'm not complaining, but I'm sorry—

ARLENE: No, no, you're right. Piece of shit.

JULIA: I'm just, I'm *new* here, I don't want to get off on the wrong foot, but—

ARLENE: Yes, well, a lot of good *that* thinking did you, eh?

(ARLENE laughs; JULIA doesn't. ARLENE indicates JULIA's injured foot. JULIA joins in the laughter, then suddenly:)

JULIA: Oh! I'm sorry—

ARLENE: What?

JULIA: —you're working, aren't you—

ARLENE: I'm—

JULIA: —and I'm disturbing your work, your, your, your—

ARLENE: I'm—

JULIA: —your *concentration*. God, I'm such a —your *process*—I'm such a, *geez*.

ARLENE (*beat*): Show's over, darling.

(Silence. JULIA looks stricken.)

JULIA: What?

ARLENE (*blinks, then*): The show's over. Audience went home. (*Beat, laughs.*) You didn't hit your head, did you?

JULIA (*laughter, possibly of relief*): Oh, oh, *oh. Oh.* (*Beat.*) I—you meant—yes, I *know* the show is over for *tonight*, yes—

ARLENE: I mean, you were there. . .

JULIA (*laughs*): . . .yes. . .

ARLENE: . . .and I was there, I saw it all. You were right there onstage.

JULIA: . . .all right, all right. . .

ARLENE: . . .said lines and everything.

(They laugh.)

JULIA: I just thought, you know, maybe you were, you know: "Coming down."

ARLENE: Ah.

JULIA: From your, from your *work*—Oh! You know what I read? Sarah Siddons, you know, when she did Lady Scottish-Play—

ARLENE: Uh-huh—

JULIA: —it would take her forever to come *down*, her, you know, her *concentration*, it was so, you know, such a, her *process*, so *amazing*, and you know what?

ARLENE: What?

JULIA: She *blushed*.

ARLENE: Ah.

JULIA: I mean, you know, she was so—*(makes a face, growls) into it,* you know, like that, she would actually *blush.* Not faking. She would *actually* blush. *(Beat.)* She couldn't stop herself.

ARLENE: Ah.

JULIA: *That's* what I want, boy. *That's.* . .I wanna be just like Sarah Siddons, I want. . .

(JULIA drifts into silence.)

ARLENE: That was Duse, darling.

(Silence.)

JULIA: It was?

ARLENE: Mm-hm.

JULIA: Not Sarah Siddons?

ARLENE *(shakes her head):* Eleonora Duse.

JULIA: Oh. *(Genuinely sad:)* I liked the name so much, too. "Sarah Siddons." *(Beat.)* Well, *shoot.*

ARLENE: Well. Anyway. I'm just waiting for Peter, so. . .

(Silence.)

JULIA: *Oh.*

ARLENE: He's coming out with us tonight.

JULIA: *Wow,* how about that, huh?

ARLENE: *Yes,* imagine? Are you coming?

JULIA: Oh, gosh, I don't know—

ARLENE: Oh, you should come out with us—

JULIA: —two nights in a row.

ARLENE: —now, come on, you left early last night—Oh! God, I forgot all about it. Your credit card.

JULIA: Ah. Well, you know—

(*ARLENE digs through her purse.*)

JULIA: —as long as we've bumped into each other like this.

ARLENE (*still searching*): What, "bumped"? We *act* together, for God's sake. Chekhov. Ensemble. We're supposed to be—where'd I—supposed to be "connected," all that shit. Why didn't you ask for it back?

JULIA: Oh, I don't like to ask.

(*Pause, as ARLENE stops searching long enough to look at JULIA. ARLENE then resumes the search and comes up with the credit card.*)

ARLENE: Here we go.

JULIA (*taking the card from ARLENE*): Great.

ARLENE (*pulls a receipt from her purse*): Just insanely generous of you, leaving your card with us.

JULIA: Oh, don't.

ARLENE: No, no, it *was*. I got home so late, Peter had already given up on me, I still had to walk his *dog*—

JULIA (*delighted*): Oh, your little dog—!

ARLENE: —well, he's Peter's, but whatever, little shit was even in our *wedding*, barked the whole goddamn time—

(*JULIA laughs.*)

ARLENE: —anyway, last night, got home, Peter was showering up to go to bed—took *forever*—when I told *him* about it, what you'd done, he just couldn't believe it. Thinks you're an angel.

JULIA: Oh, no.

ARLENE (*hands the receipt to JULIA*): Insanely generous, I mean it.

JULIA: It was nothing, we only had—

ARLENE: —well, yes, but after you *left*, then we stayed for *hours*—

(*Silence. JULIA is looking at the receipt. Her mouth works, but she's not speaking. Finally:*)

JULIA: Wow.

ARLENE: My goodness, did we—? (*Pause.*) Did we overstep?

(*Hold: JULIA looks at the receipt. ARLENE looks at JULIA. Lights snap to black.*)

*

II

There Should Be Something We Can Do

(*Lights up; a few moments later. JULIA sits, as before, just staring at the receipt. ARLENE paces.*)

ARLENE: My God. (*Pause.*) My *God*. (*Pause.*) I *told* them. Tried to, anyway. (*Pause.*) Fucking *actors*. Pizza takes too long? Never mind, we'll just eat our *young*. (*Pause.*) What a tribe. (*Pause.*) My God, how. . .?

JULIA (*a little numb, the word sounds like a moan*): . . . how. . .

ARLENE: . . .oh. . .

JULIA: . . .how am I going to pay. . . ?

ARLENE: I know. I know. On what you make here, I feel, I feel *awful* about. . .*No* one knows how you do it. Any of you, whatever your. . . category is, I've never grasped how in the *world* . . . (*Silence.*) I figured— (*Giggles at her own stupidity.*) I figured you were *moneyed*, some*thing*. . .

JULIA: Oh my God, no. My mom. . .

(*JULIA makes a helpless gesture. Silence.*)

ARLENE: *What* a bunch of. . .pigs we are.

JULIA: I didn't. . .I didn't think. . .You guys were just, you said, you were just going to get *coffee*. Maybe, you know. An appetizer.

ARLENE: Or dessert, yes—

JULIA: —or *dessert*, yes, something. . .

(*Silence.*)

ARLENE: Well—you did *say*—

(*Silence. JULIA looks at* ARLENE.)

JULIA: Yes.

ARLENE: I mean, you know, I, *I* for one, just speaking for *me*—

JULIA: Oh, I know—

ARLENE: —*I* figured, "Well, she wouldn't have offered if it was a problem—"

JULIA: —no, I know. That's true. It's *my*—I just— (*Shrugs. Pause.*) Okay. Okay, well, I should go.

ARLENE: You're not coming out?

JULIA: No, no, I—

ARLENE: Oh, you must. Listen, we'll work it out. We'll take up a collection, we'll just say to everyone—

JULIA: No, no, no—

ARLENE: —"Hey, ya fuckin' swine, did you have to chew through her kids' college educations?"

(*ARLENE laughs. JULIA stands, smiles, near tears.*)

JULIA: I'm not—I don't have kids yet.

ARLENE (*pause*): I know. It was just a joke.

JULIA: Right, okay, I'm going to—

ARLENE: Oh, come on, this is killing me. Stand *up* for yourself. We, come *on*, we took advantage, there should be *some*thing we can do. (*Beat.*) I insist. You must come out with us. Give us another chance. We "Ruling Class," eh? Just because you're *young*, just because you're *new*. . .? (*Beat.*) And what about Peter?

JULIA (*coming out of a fog*): Hm?

ARLENE: *Yes.* (*Pause.*) Peter. (*Pause.*) What about him? He'll be crushed. He never comes out, I should know, the old stick-in-the-mud, I sleep with him, he *never*—listen, he's over at the joint now, talking to the manager about a table. For all of us. *All* of us, yes? When I told him, do you know, when I told him last night about what you did, this *insanely*—he was just, you know, he was just bowled over. "That girl," he said. "That new girl. Talk about, talk about *instincts.*"

JULIA: He said that?

ARLENE: Yes, and then he said, "You guys going out *tomorrow* night? After our show?" I said, "Whattayou care, you *artist*, you—"

(*JULIA laughs.*)

ARLENE: And believe this: he *sparkled.* Honestly.

JULIA: Oh, I just love acting with him. Those *eyes.*

ARLENE: And he puts this finger to his lips—

JULIA (*smiles*): Oh, yes—

ARLENE: —like he does, he says: (*pause, as she nods slowly, then*) "Maybe I'll go."

(*They both laugh.*)

ARLENE: And then, and *then*, he says "I'll go over to the joint, talk to the *other* guy, I'll get us the *nice* table—"

JULIA: Ohh. . .

ARLENE: . . .in the *back*, going to use his *"influence.* . ."

(*JULIA laughs and claps delightedly.*)

ARLENE: . . .big *star*, you know?

(*They both laugh affectionately, and it falls into silence.*)

ARLENE: Oh! And this is *just* between you and me, *nobody* else knows about this, so my *God,* don't say anything, but Peter's making an announcement tonight—

JULIA: Oh, about the new space, *yes!* That's so exciting!

(*Silence.*)

ARLENE (*looks at JULIA*): Ah. (*Pause.*) Well, then.

(*A gesture from ARLENE, perhaps just a shrug and a smile. Hold. Lights out.*)

*

III

I Never Know What It Means

(*Lights up on ARLENE and JULIA. ARLENE has the receipt. JULIA is stretching her injured leg.*)

JULIA: You're going to be late. You should just go. Have a good time.

ARLENE: No. No. We can do something here. I mean, look, I feel responsible. Somewhat.

JULIA: Oh, no—

ARLENE: No, I do. (*Beat*). I mean, yes, you *did* offer—

JULIA: I did, I know—

ARLENE: —some people might have an *opinion* of that. (*Shrugs; pause.*) I mean, *I* think you're sweet. Somebody *else*? "Who's the idiot?"

JULIA: I know—

ARLENE: You see? This is a strange profession. You have to watch your back. Gotta know who your friends are, or you're fucked.

JULIA: Yes.

ARLENE: All right: The cheese platter. *I* never saw it, it sure didn't come down to *my* end of the table. So: We'll just tell ol' Wisconsin *Bob*—oh.

JULIA: What?

ARLENE: Never mind. We can't do that.

JULIA: Right. (*Pause.*) Because Bob's from Wisconsin.

ARLENE (*pause*): Bob's not from Wisconsin. He just thinks "wine and cheese" is its own food group, right?

JULIA: Ah.

ARLENE: Makes you curse that fuckin' unisex bathroom, I'll tell you that much. (*Pause.*) It was. . .just a "cheese joke." (*Pause.*) 'Cause he likes—he—never mind—

JULIA: Oh.

ARLENE: *Anyway*: He's "struggling."

(*ARLENE makes a drinking gesture.*)

JULIA: *Oh.*

ARLENE: I mean, we have to understand about *some* things.

JULIA: Right.

ARLENE: So. You're okay with the platter. You'll buy that.

JULIA: Oh. Sure.

(*Pause, as JULIA stretches and ARLENE reads.*)

ARLENE: There are *twelve* salads here. *Twelve.*

JULIA: Really? That's. . .that's a lot of salad.

ARLENE: There are only *eight* people in the cast, for chrissakes, *you* weren't even there, chrissakes, *Peter* wasn't there, who ordered all the fuckin' salads?

JULIA: I don't know who ordered them. (*Pause.*) I wasn't there.

(*ARLENE makes a "tsk" sound. Pause. ARLENE watches JULIA stretch.*)

ARLENE: You know what you are?

JULIA: What?

ARLENE: You're *nubile.*

JULIA (*smiles shyly*): Oh. You. (*Beat.*) What...what is that? You know, can I tell you something?

ARLENE: Yes.

JULIA: I've heard that word all my life—nu—

ARLENE: (*With her:*) —"nubile," uh-huh—

JULIA: —and I've never known what it means, and you know what?

ARLENE: What?

JULIA: I always forget to look it up.

(*Silence.*)

ARLENE: Uh-huh.

JULIA: I have to look up words every single day, right? But that one: I always forget. And so, when someone calls me that, I just smile—you know, like I just did—

ARLENE: Yes.

JULIA: —but that's only because *most* of the time, when I hear it, I think it must be a compliment. But that's just my guess. I have no idea.

(*Silence.*)

153

ARLENE: Well. So. The question is, "Who bought the rabbit food?"

JULIA: I—wait—

ARLENE: —"we're hunting wabbits"—

JULIA: —do—do you—is— (*Silence.*) That was a compliment, right?

(*Silence. ARLENE looks at JULIA, not unkindly.*)

ARLENE: Yes. It was a compliment.

JULIA: Thank you.

ARLENE: Welcome.

(*JULIA goes back to stretching, ARLENE goes back to the receipt.*)

ARLENE: All *right*, errant salads, dastardly table squatters, *some*body is gonna pay—oh.

JULIA: What?

ARLENE: Damn. (*Pause. Helpless gesture.*) The salad money is lost.

JULIA: Oh. (*Pause.*) Why?

ARLENE: Well, think about it.

(*Silence, as JULIA thinks. After a few moments, JULIA smiles at ARLENE, wan; shakes her head.*)

ARLENE: Well, how are we supposed to get to the bottom of it? Eh? Who do we go to? You see? (*Pause.*) Eh?

JULIA: *Ohh.* (*Pause. Smiles, wan; puts her head in her hands.*)

ARLENE: Look: So-and-so, say *Liz*, we go to Liz, we say, "Liz: who was at the table with you last night? Who was with you last night?"

(*JULIA raises her head; she and ARLENE look at each other.*)

ARLENE: "Who was with you last night?"

JULIA: (*Pause.*) I don't know.

ARLENE: (*Pause.*) All right. Let's run with that. She *might* say, "I don't know," she might *say* that. But do we believe her? That she doesn't know? Maybe she was just too *drunk* to know? Or maybe she really *doesn't* know. Maybe she didn't have a salad at all, maybe she was gone to the restroom when the goddamn salads were ordered in the *first* fuckin' place.

JULIA: *Right.*

ARLENE: Or maybe: (*Pause.*) Maybe she knows we're on to her.

(*Pause.*)

JULIA: Uh-huh.

ARLENE: In which case, the bitter, brutal *truth*, if it comes to it, hey, she's in show business, she's obviously broke, she knows some moron—sorry—handed over her credit card so hey, she orders some *salad*, what did she do that everybody else *didn't*, what do we *expect* she'll say back to us? (*Pause. Waits for JULIA to answer, then:*) She'll lie!

JULIA: Ohhh!

ARLENE: She'll lie her tight little ass off.

JULIA: Uh-huh.

ARLENE: You've seen her, those *pants*—

JULIA (*whispers*): Oh, I know.

ARLENE: —like she's *poured* into them.

JULIA (*whispers*): I *know*. . .

(*The two women giggle conspiratorially. Pause.*)

ARLENE: No, the "Liz Situation," it's. . . (*Beat.*) It's untenable.

(*Pause. JULIA looks at ARLENE, as though to speak.*)

ARLENE: Yes, dear?

(*JULIA smiles, shakes her head shyly, goes back to stretching. ARLENE reads the receipt. Silence.*)

ARLENE (*attention on the receipt*): "Incapable of being defended—"

JULIA (*enormous relief*): *Thank* you!

(*Silence, as they go back to their routines. ARLENE grunts.*)

ARLENE: Now, this bar bill.

JULIA: I know.

ARLENE: You see what's on here. Shit I never heard of. What's the matter with a beer? Huh. Some, I mean, I'm sorry, somebody like you, I'm sorry, I don't mean. . . anything, but, all right, "unschooled" person—

JULIA: No—right—

ARLENE: —says, "Hey, take my kindness." And they do what?

JULIA: —right—

ARLENE: "Let's find the most expensive shit at the bar," look at this, "Neopolitan liqueur," some shit from *Italy*, probably, costs a fortune—

JULIA (*stretching*): Oh, no, you know what? Peter told me that stuff is cheap if you compare it to Galliano.

(*Silence. JULIA stops stretching, looks at ARLENE. Beat. ARLENE goes back to the receipt.*)

ARLENE: Ah. You're right. Not bad at all. Then I assume you're all right. You're all right with what you've done here. (*Pause; looks at JULIA.*) Leave the cheap Neopolitan liqueur on here? Don't worry about it?

JULIA: (*Beat.*) Don't worry about it.

(*ARLENE turns her attention back to the receipt. JULIA stands still.*)

ARLENE (*attention on the receipt, muses*): Yep. Compared to. . . (*Beat.*) So: The great Neopolitan-Galliano question. Just knew there was *some*thing keeping me awake at night. Lovely to have it all settled.

(*Silence.*)

ARLENE: When, exactly, did Peter elucidate you? (*Pause; looks at JULIA.*) When, exactly, did Peter elucidate you?

(*Hold: Count five. Lights out.*)

*

IV

Is It Possible?

(*JULIA sits on the stool. ARLENE is again pacing, a cell phone to her ear.*)

ARLENE: Assholes.

JULIA: I think—

ARLENE: "Please listen closely as our menu options have changed." Assholes.

JULIA: You don't have to help—

ARLENE (*stronger than she expects*): "Help?" *"Help?"* (*Beat, as ARLENE jabs at a button on the cell phone.*) There *is* no help. There's no help for *anything,* is there? (*Beat.*) They're not going to answer. (*Keeps pacing.*) Nothing for it. Should've known. Look at the time. If there's anybody there at all, they're sound asleep at the switch. You'll just have to call on Monday. Report it yourself, as a, I don't know, as a *theft* or something. (*Snorts.*)

JULIA: But it's not theft, I gave you guys my card, I said, "*Hey*"—

ARLENE: You did, yes you did—

JULIA: "—take my kindness."

(*ARLENE hands JULIA the cell phone.*)

ARLENE: Here's your—look—just make the call—

JULIA: Oh, wait, no—

ARLENE: OH, FUCK 'EM, YOU THINK THEY CARE ABOUT *YOU?! ANY* OF 'EM?

JULIA (*holding out the phone*)**:** That's not what I—this is—

ARLENE (*gathering her things*)**:** (. . .fucking *set* dressing. . .)

JULIA: Where are you going?

ARLENE: Away.

JULIA: You're not going out—?

ARLENE (*overlapping*)**:** (. . .might as well talk to a *foot*stool. . .)

JULIA: —Peter said he was going to—

ARLENE: I know what Peter said, he's my fucking husband, I know what he says and what he doesn't say. Oh *boy*, do I know what he doesn't say.

(*Silence. ARLENE pats her pockets.*)

ARLENE: Where's my phone? I have to call Peter, where's my phone?

(*JULIA holds out the cell phone that ARLENE handed her. ARLENE snatches the phone and dashes it to the ground. She stomps on it, smashing it into pieces. Spits on it.*)

ARLENE: I want *my* phone! I want *my* phone! I want to talk to *my* husband! Now where is *my* phone?! Eh? Do you know *that*? You "intellectual?" Do you know where *my* phone is? You *simp!* Do you know where *my* phone is?

(*Beat. JULIA slowly points to the destroyed phone on the floor. ARLENE stands, looking at the smashed phone, breathless.*)

ARLENE: Oh.

JULIA: (*Pause.*) That's what I—

ARLENE: Shut up.

(*ARLENE goes to her knees and begins scooping the pieces of the phone into her purse. JULIA pulls out her own phone, taps the passcode, and gently offers it to ARLENE. Pause. ARLENE takes the phone.*)

ARLENE: Thank you.

(*ARLENE dials. In the pause, she looks at JULIA and is about to speak, when the phone is answered. ARLENE reacts silently to what is said on the other end, then:*)

ARLENE (*at phone*): Eh— (*Beat.*) Stop. Stop. *Stop.* It's not her. (*Beat.*) *It's not her.* It's me.

(*JULIA gasps.*)

ARLENE (to *JULIA*): Yeah. Yeah, *another* brilliant stroke. Next time, tell me to use the *green room* phone, you. . . hairless *slit.* (*Back at phone:*) What? (*Pause.*) Oh, well, she offered me a kindness, my phone is, you know. Dead. (*Pause.*) *Dead.* Do *you* need a definition? It's *dead.* (*Pause.*) No, I will *not* be home, that's why I'm calling you, I will *not* be home tonight, I *have* no home, so *you* can walk your fat-snouted *cur* in the morning and explain to *him* why the world suddenly looks so different.

(*ARLENE jabs at the phone, ending the call. Long silence.*)

JULIA: I'm sorry.

ARLENE (*an instant reaction*): Whattaya sorry about?

(*ARLENE suddenly grabs JULIA by the hair and jams the receipt in her face.*)

ARLENE: What're *you* sorry about? Huh? I *swindled* you! HAH! I ordered everything *on* here, you *fool,* you you you NINNY! (*Points to something on the receipt.*) This thing? This "French thing"? I TOOK IT HOME! I FED IT TO THAT GODDAMNED DOG! And you stand here and, what, *you're* sorry? *I* should be sorry! *I* should be sorry!

ARLENE (*cont'd*)**:** You understand? *I AM THE ONE WHO'S SORRY!*

(*ARLENE suddenly slaps JULIA across the face, knocking her to the floor. ARLENE unleashes an enormous scream of pain and loss. Her legs buckle and she sits on the floor, spent, some distance away from JULIA. Silence.*)

ARLENE: How long I've been with this company. . .how long I've been in this *business*. . .how long I've been— (*Pause.*) Three months ago, I didn't even know you were on the goddamn *planet* and *NOW LOOK AT ME!* (*Pause.*) How did you *do* this to me?

(*ARLENE looks at JULIA, shakes her head.*)

ARLENE: I find it very difficult to look at you. Perhaps you understand.

JULIA: I do.

ARLENE: I look at you, and I think—is it even possible? Is it possible for one person to be so . . .naive. So monumentally, catastrophically stupid? Is that even possible?

(*Silence.*)

JULIA: Yes. (*Pause.*) Yes, it's possible.

(*Hold. Lights to black.*)

END OF PLAY

James Serpento

Lazy Susan

An Inconsequential Meditation
in One Scene

inspired by
"The Night Before the Trial"

as translated by R. Andrew White
with Jane Martsinovsky Hendricks

and one or two other things

Lazy Susan was first presented by Mad Genie Productions in Chicago, IL in March, 1994. It was directed by Christine Hartman. The cast was as follows:

HE	David Mitchell Ghilardi
SHE	Tricia Kym Armstrong
A STRANGER	R. Andrew White

CHARACTERS

HE

SHE

A STRANGER

SETTING

Some interior landscape. And a living room.

James Serpento

Lazy Susan
An Inconsequential Meditation in One Scene

inspired by "The Night Before the Trial"
by Anton Chekhov

as translated by R. Andrew White
with Jane Martsinovky Hendricks

(*HE and SHE in chairs. HE reads a newspaper, SHE reads a
book. Between them, on a table, is a lazy susan, filled with
candies. Silence, as they read. HE turns the page of his
newspaper. SHE takes a candy from the lazy susan, unwraps
it noisily, and pops it into her mouth. SHE sucks on it loudly
for a few seconds, then crunches it for a few seconds, then
swallows. SHE turns a page of her book and has reached the
end. SHE rotates the lazy susan, reaches for another candy,
is about to unwrap it, then stops. Silence. SHE turns the page
back, looks for something, doesn't find it. SHE turns to the
final page again and runs her finger down it, quickly re-
reading it. Silence. SHE puts the candy back in the lazy
susan.*)

SHE: There's something wrong with this book.

HE (*doesn't look up from his paper*)**:** Hm?

SHE: I said, there's something wrong with this book. It's
defective or something.

HE: How's that?

SHE: There's this last line, "I wonder what will happen," then there's this question mark, and then there's nothing.

HE *(buried in the newspaper, reading)*: LeBron James is *so* rich. . .

SHE: Did you hear what I said?

HE *(ibid)*: . . .I could live for a year on what he loses in the sofa cushions. . .

SHE: *There is something wrong with this book!*

(A beat, as HE calmly puts his paper down.)

HE: All right. There's something wrong with your book.

SHE: I adore Chekhov. I mean, I absolutely *love, adore, worship* Chekhov. And here I sit with this book of Chekhov, I get to this last piece, I get to the last page of the last piece and—

(SHE noisily unwraps another piece of candy. As she does:)

SHE: —I want to know why someone would tear the last page out of a book! I want to know what could possibly induce whatever sick, twisted individual to do something like that, to drive someone absolutely dip-banana by doing something like that. I *mean*. . .

(SHE stuffs the candy into her mouth, defiant. SHE puts her book down, helpless. SHE sits motionless for a moment, and there is just the sound of her noisily sucking on her piece of candy.)

HE: You're in your "I want a divorce" pose again. *(Pause.)* Maybe that's all there is.

(SHE looks at him, crunches her candy, a bit like a squirrel.)

HE: You know? Maybe that's all that was written, sort of a, I don't know, a *Twilight Zone* story, you know, that's all there is, you just have to *imagine* whatever way it ends.

SHE *(just looks at him; then)*: How long have we been married?

HE: Six years.

SHE: Then you know how an answer like that would infuriate me.

(The doorbell rings. SHE throws a candy at him.)

HE: I'll get that.

(HE exits. SHE just sits, her head in her hands, staring at the book.)

SHE: Oh, *man . . .*

(A STRANGER enters. SHE yelps with surprise.)

STRANGER: Don't be alarmed.

SHE: Where's my husband?

STRANGER: You don't have one anymore.

(SHE stares at him. Then:)

SHE: Oh.

STRANGER: May I sit?

SHE: Yes, thank you.

STRANGER: You're welcome.

(They both sit. Beat.)

SHE: You've killed him, then.

STRANGER *(laughing)***:** Oh, no.

SHE: Oh. *(Pause.)* Candy?

(SHE slowly, nervously, rotates the lazy susan.)

SHE: I would offer you something to drink, all we have in the house is water—

(SHE stops short, gazing into the lazy susan.)

SHE: Oh, my God.

STRANGER: Are you all right?

SHE: You're a burglar. Aren't you.

STRANGER: My good woman, do I look li—

SHE: Or a mass murderer, or something, aren't you. You're going to, you're going to, you're going to. . .

STRANGER: Finish, there, there. . .

SHE: . . .you're going to hhhhhhhuuuuuuurrrrrt me. Aren't you. They won't find me for days and days and the mice will have gotten to me and. . . right?

STRANGER: Nope.

SHE: Oh.

(SHE rotates the lazy susan, a little more quickly.)

SHE: You're going to, you're going to, you're going to. . .

STRANGER: Finish, there, there. . .

SHE: . . .you're going to. . .

(SHE stops the lazy susan, staring into the tray.)

SHE: . . .make love to me. *(SHE removes a candy.)* You're gonna do it. You're gonna Do It. You're gonna. . . you're going to. . .*excite* me, you're going to gently open my blouse. . . *(unwraps the candy, noisily)* . . .and place a hand very carefully near my heart. *(Pops the candy into her mouth.)* Which just so happens to be near an erogenous area. *(Gives a long, juicy suck on the candy; delectable.)* You're going to breathe against my neck, and the temperature of your breath will be perfect– *(a gasp)* –and I shall swoon into your arms, collapse against you so you can feel my *plumpness*, and you shall throw open the gates of my passion and the horses will run, they will *run, oh yes,* they will run run *ruuun deep deeep deeeep* into the night, their cries, their cries *rise riiise riiiiise* to the moon. . . *(breathless)* . . .like music's ghosts. . .

(Beat. The STRANGER makes a sound like a dripping faucet.)

STRANGER: LeBron James is *so* rich. . .

(Silence.)

SHE: What did you say?

STRANGER: . . .I could live for a year on what he loses in the sofa cushions. . .

SHE: My husband said that!

STRANGER: That doesn't make it any less true.

(Silence.)

SHE: You're not gonna. . .are you. I mean, the. . . love thing. *(Pause.)* Shit.

(SHE throws the licked piece of candy back into the lazy susan.)

SHE: I can't think. . . *(As SHE spins the lazy susan more quickly:)* You're going to, you're going to, you're going to. . .

STRANGER *(overlapping)*: Finish (there, there). . .

SHE: . . .you're going to. . .

(SHE stops the rotation and studies a tray.)

SHE:. . .take me on a journey. *(Pause. Then, joyfully:)* Now I have you, you sly dog!

STRANGER *(laughing)*: I never could fool you.

SHE: Egypt and France and Belgium and Guam, on a nickel a day, a dime if there's time, just a quarter to the border, and a cent for the rent. We'll be mysterious to everyone. Everyone will want to know who we are, for it is clear we're not like the natives. We'll prowl the alleys at night, looking for evil-doers—

STRANGER: —Russian spies—

SHE: —Russian *spies* and Henry Mancini music will play underneath it all—

(Silence. She stares at the STRANGER in stunned, quiet terror; then:)

SHE: Eh? *(Pause; then, suddenly jovial:)* Hah! You bet your bottom backseat on—that's not right.

STRANGER: There, there. . .

SHE: That's not right.

STRANGER: There, there. . .

SHE: Your bottom bucket. . . *(Pause.)* Your bottom buckshot. . . *(Pause.)* Your bottom buck. *(Pause.)* Buck. Dollar. Bottom dollar! You bet your bottom—

STRANGER: Too late.

SHE: Oh, come on.

STRANGER: You blew it.

SHE: Oh, no!

STRANGER: Moment killer.

SHE: No journey?

STRANGER: It's spoilt now.

SHE: Oh, no. . .

STRANGER: 'Fraid so. . .

SHE: Just Egypt? *(Pause.)* How 'bout Guam? *(Pause.)* What Cheer, Iowa?

STRANGER: There's really a town called What Cheer, Iowa?

SHE: Oh, yes! I was looking at a map, I was looking at all the various places that we could go—

STRANGER: —you and your husband—

SHE: —yes. . . *(Coyly:)* Or whoever. . .

(She spins the lazy susan, a bit more quickly.)

SHE: And right smack dapple in the idly piddly middly of that crab-apple mapple is, what do you know, hey diddly doh, why, it's What Cheer, Ioway, come to play but you'll wanna stay. . .

STRANGER: . . . cause you need to get away. . .

(She begins spinning the lazy susan very fast.)

SHE: . . .deserve a break today, I deserve a break today, if I don't get a break today, I'm gonna, I'm gonna, I'm gonna. . .

STRANGER: Finish, (there, there). . .

SHE: . . .I'm gonna—

(SHE gives the lazy susan one last spin and candies go flying all over the floor. Silence. HE enters.)

HE: There was no one there. *(Of the candies on the floor:)* What *is* all this?

SHE: He can't see you?

STRANGER: No.

SHE: Well, you'll pardon me, but that's very clichéd.

STRANGER: I try.

SHE: Hey! You said I didn't have a husband anymore!

STRANGER: You don't. He's not your husband.

SHE: You're not my husband?

HE: Nope. Not anymore.

SHE: Huh. When did that happen?

HE: When you did this:

(HE demonstrates, taking the same head-in-the-hands pose SHE used previously.)

SHE: Wow. That's some power.

STRANGER: Stronger by the hour.

HE *(picking up a candy)***:** Why, you're capable of anything, aren't you.

(A brief, awkward silence. SHE seems momentarily ashamed. Then:)

SHE: What does all this have to do with my book? The fact that some loon-joon stole the last few pages out of my book, I'm being *punished?*

STRANGER: Who's punishing you?

SHE: *You* are. The two of you are. You're confiscating me.

HE: I don't think that's possible, is it?

(STRANGER shakes his head at HE, conspiratorially.)

SHE: All I did was make an observation, all I said was, "Golly golly gee, who had this book before me?"

HE: That isn't how you said it.

SHE: Well, no, but—

HE: I mean, with all the rhyme and all that, come on, I mean, you weren't nearly so interesting then, were you?

(Silence.)

SHE: You bastard.

HE: I'm just saying—

SHE *(overlapping)***:** —try to *improve* myself. . . *(A long pause.)* Shit.

STRANGER: "—*albeit*—"

SHE: —*albeit* (thank you) in little ways, like, okay, maybe *talking* a little bit differently, like, okay, like, okay, like, okay—

STRANGER: —*Finish!* There, *there!*

(Silence.)

SHE: Okay. Okay. I wanna stop now.

STRANGER: All right.

SHE: No, I mean, I mean, I know that's my line and then that was your line, but I mean I really wanna stop now, okay? I don't think this is working.

STRANGER *(with a fixed, nervous smile)*: I think we're doing just fine.

SHE: No, no, no! I'm just delivering my, I don't know, my *programmed response* or something. What I *want* to say is somehow the same as what I'm *supposed* to say here, but that's a fluke, it's a cheesecloth fact, and I want to stop. *(Looks at the audience.)* Okay? Can we stop? You don't mind, right, this is. . .this is. . . *(Silence. Looks at the STRANGER.)* That's it. That's all we have. I'm stopping the thing. I'm stopping it. *(Looks at the audience, smiles disarmingly.)* I'm stopping it. *And:* This is all rehearsed. This was all planned.

(STRANGER glances nervously at the audience.)

SHE: See that? That little look he just gave you, like *I'm* crazy or something, like *I'm* out of control? That was planned. He did that last night too, just like that. He didn't deviate one little bit. *(Pause.)* You see? *Not one little bit! (Pause.)* It's a bit! It's a *bit!* (*To the* STRANGER:) *I'm blowin' the whistle! I'm singin' like a canary! YOU'LL NEVER WORK IN THIS TOWN AGAIN!*

STRANGER: Are you all right?

SHE: You rehearsed that!

STRANGER: Just calm down.

HE: What's the matter with her?

SHE: You rehearsed that too!

STRANGER: Does she always act like this?

SHE: You rehearsed that! You rehearsed that!

HE *(to the STRANGER)***:** I don't know, it's some "technique."

SHE: *YOU REHEARSED THAT!*

HE *(to the STRANGER)***:** Meisner, something—

STRANGER: *Ah!*

(SHE squawks like a huge bird and runs around the room, flapping her arms.)

SHE: *YOU REHEARSED THAT! YOU REHEARSED THAT!*

STRANGER *(pointing offstage)***:** No, *you* rehearsed *that!*

SHE *(pointing offstage in the opposite direction)***:** No, *you* rehearsed *that!*

HE *(points offstage in two directions)***:** No, *you* rehearsed— *(Beat, then:)* Do you hear a baby crying?

(Dead stop. SHE launches herself at HE, the STRANGER trying to subdue her.)

SHE: You *fuck*—!

HE: See ya—!

SHE: —you miserable *fuck*—!!

HE *(exiting hurriedly)***:** —wouldn't wanna *be* ya!

SHE *(utterly hysterical)***:** *WHERE'S HE GOING?!*

STRANGER *(with seeming compassion)***:** Ssh, there, there, now—

SHE *(after HE)***:** *YOU'RE A MISERABLE FUCKING ACTOR! YOU NEVER TOLD THE TRUTH ONSTAGE ONE MISERABLE MINUTE!*

STRANGER *(concerned)***:** Easy now—

SHE *(of HE)***:** BUT HE'S *LYING!!*

STRANGER *(calm)***:** All right. . .

SHE: You know that. He's lying. *(Pause. Moves toward the STRANGER)*. Good. You know. You love me, you know—you know that he's—

(The STRANGER sits, makes the dripping faucet sound, stopping HER in her tracks.)

SHE *(eyes wide with terror and shame, filling with tears)*: Fuck.

(HE re-enters.)

HE: The producer wants to know what's going on.

SHE: Please. *Please.* We *did* all this. It's the same as before, you rehearsed that, this very same thing, this is a motherlode of *shit*—

HE: What's that?

SHE: A *motherlode*—

HE: Come again?

SHE: A *motherlo*— *(Pause.)* A mother of. . . *(Pause.)* A mother. . . *(Pause.)* Oh, my God. . .

STRANGER: Ssssh, now. . .

SHE: Everyone's looking at me.

HE: They're *supposed* to, you're *acting*—

SHE: *Shut up! (Pause.)* I. . .okay. Right. Right.

(Silence.)

SHE: I'm crazy, aren't I. I am. *(Pause.)* I'm really. . .I'm really. . .This is very uncomfortable.

STRANGER: Do you want to sit down?

SHE *(to HE)*: We're not really married.

HE: No.

SHE *(to the audience)*: We're not really married.

HE *(turning to the audience)*: On the night of February 14th . . .

SHE: . . .Valentine's Day. . .

HE: . . .don'tcha know. . .

SHE *(head bowed, spent)*: . . .all bloody rehearsed, you prick. . .

HE: . . .this woman, the woman you see here. . .

SHE *(head bowed, raises her hand)*: . . .that would be me. . .

HE: . . .walked out to her automobile. . .

SHE *(very quietly)*: . . .vroom, vroom, bang the garage door. . .

HE: . . .she removed the carseat from the backseat. . .

SHE *(sing-song)*: . . .repeat, repeat. . .

HE: . . .and brought it into the house. She carefully placed the carseat on its back in the bathtub. . .

SHE: . . .flubba lubba lubba. . .

HE: . . .gently strapped her tiny child into the carseat. And turned on the bathwater. . .

(She keeps her head bowed, rocks back and forth.)

SHE: . . .not too hot and not too cold for you're not even one year old. . .

HE: . . .the baby in the carseat on the bottom of the bathtub, staring up at the ceiling as the waves approach—

SHE *(a pathetic roar)*: You're gauche, you're gauche, you smell like a roach!!

HE: . . .then she sat down to read, with one light on and one light off. . .

SHE *(dreamily)*: . . .and oh, how I love that Mister Chekhov . . .

HE: . . .listening always to the rush of the water. . .

SHE: . . .like Niagara, never ever been but oh how I oughtta. . .

HE: . . .and that's all.

(Pause. Her breathing is audible: heavy and measured.)

STRANGER: The Russian lady who lives downstairs. . .

HE: Oh, yes. . .

STRANGER: . . .she brought up a book. . .

SHE: . . .oh how I love that Mister Chekhov. . .

HE: . . .just so. . .

SHE: From the library, she says. But I got her number. And a laugh at her expense. She knocked on my door and when there was no answer, she opened my door and stepped inside. . .

HE: . . .you there in the chair, half-light a-bathing soft your hair. . .

SHE: . . .stepped into the puddle of water that was spreading along the floor now. Quiet locusts now. . . *(Pause. Giggles. Then:)* "Vhat ees dees? Susie? Vere is da baby?"
And there was quiet, for a moment, as she looked there inside.

(Quiet, for a moment.)

SHE: Then her eyes, very close and lo, full of brine
Her eyes very close, oh very close, lo, to mine and— *(Beat.)*
"Vhat haf yoo done?! *(Beat.)*
"Vhat haf yoo done to da *baby*?!" *(Beat.)*
Ah yoo aht ahf yoo maighnt? *(Chuckles quietly.)*
Ah yoo aht ahf yoo maighnt?
Ah yoo aht ahf yoo maighnt?"

(She repeats the phrase quietly under the next few lines.)

HE: I'd forgotten about the Russian lady.

STRANGER: Momentary lapse.

HE *(pause)*: Is there any more to do here?

STRANGER: Nope.

HE: It was good tonight.

STRANGER: I think so.

HE: Are they late with the music?

STRANGER: Not till the end.

HE: Ah. Drink?

STRANGER *(lustily)*: Vodka!

HE: Capital!

STRANGER: Lead on!

(The men start to exit. The STRANGER pauses, addresses the audience, referring to the candy that is on the floor:)

STRANGER: Do help yourselves.

(SHE is alone.)

SHE: Ah yoo aht ahf yoo maighnt?
Ah yoo aht ahf yoo maighnt?
Ah yoo aht ahf yoo maighnt?

(Recording of "a waltz heard in the distance" kicks in, complete with "tape wow."

VOICE FROM THE SOUND BOOTH: Sorry!

(Tears are rolling down HER cheeks as She answers in her Russian accent:)

SHE: Dat's ahlright, dahlink.
Dat's ahlright.
Daaahhhht's ahlright.

(Lights snap to black.)

END OF PLAY

R. Andrew White

A Happy End

a short play

from the short story of the same title
by Anton Chekhov

as translated by R. Andrew White

This adaptation of *A Happy End* was presented by Valparaiso University, Valparaiso, IN in February, 2000. It was directed by R. Andrew White. The costume designs were by Ann Kessler, and the set design was by Alan Stalmah. The cast was as follows:

LYUBOV GRIGORYEVNA	Vanessa Hughes
STYCHKIN	John Steven Paul

CHARACTERS

LYÚBOV GRIGÓRYEVNA, a matchmaker

NIKOLÁY NIKOLÁYICH STÝCHKIN, a bachelor and railroad employee, 52 years old

SETTING
The action takes place in the parlor of Stychkin's home.

R. Andrew White

A Happy End

a short play

from the short story of the same title
by Anton Chekhov

as translated by R. Andrew White

*(Lights come up on the parlor of chief-conductor
STYCHKIN's home. STYCHKIN enters with a large platter of
food—cheese, bread, kielbasa, pickles, herring, and the
like—which he places on a table. The coat of his uniform
hangs open; his shirt is wrinkled, and his collar is undone.
He exits and enters again with a bottle of vodka and two
shot glasses, which he places next to the food.*

A loud, persistent knock at the door.)

STYCHKIN: Yes, yes. . . coming!

*(Another knock. STYCHKIN opens the door, and we see
LYUBOV GRIGORYEVNA. She looks STYCHKIN up and down.)*

LYUBOV: Well, you didn't have to get all dressed up just for
me.

STYCHKIN: Hm? Oh!

*(He looks himself over and makes a feeble effort to
straighten his clothes.)*

STYCHKIN: I'm sorry, I just was. . .

LYUBOV: I mean you have to give me something to *work* with here.

STYCHKIN: Yes, yes, of course. I'm off duty today.

LYUBOV: So I see.

STYCHKIN: Well, I. . .I'm most happy to make your acquaintance. Semyón Iványch recommended you on the point that you may be able to offer assistance in a delicate matter of. . .of great importance. I have, Lyubov Grigoryevna, reached the age of fifty-two—that time of life when most people have sent their grown children into the world. Now, mind you, I have a secure place in society, a stable job. And as an employee of the railroad, I earn enough to feed a wife and children. My fortune is not large, let's be frank about that, but between you and me, I have money in the bank which my chosen lifestyle has allowed me to save.

LYUBOV: I'm not surprised.

STYCHKIN: At any rate, I am down-to-earth, sober, I lead a life of consistency and sensibility. I hold myself as an example among men. But . . .

LYUBOV: Yes?

STYCHKIN: . . .one thing I do lack. A partner. A life partner. It's true. I wander the earth like a gypsy, from place to place, never finding satisfaction nor a place to call home. When I'm ill, there's no one to bring me water, and so on. But apart from all that, a married man, well, he carries more weight in society, you must agree.

LYUBOV: Sure.

STYCHKIN: Now, I'm an educated man, with money, but if you look at me, I mean *really* look at me, what am I? A man with no one. No family. Might as well be a priest. And so I wish very much to enter into the bonds of Hymen—that is, to enter into matrimony with some worthy person.

LYUBOV: A fine thing!

STYCHKIN: But I know no one. In this town, in *every* town people are strangers to me. Where can I go, to whom can I apply? Well, that's your job, eh? I mean Semyón Iványch said you were a specialist in these matters. Since arranging the happiness of others is your profession, I beg you, Lyubov Grigoryevna, help me to arrange my future, my happiness. You know all of the eligible young ladies in this town. I know you can accommodate me.

LYUBOV: That's possible. . .

STYCHKIN *(pours out two shots of vodka)*: Eat something. I humbly beg you.

LYUBOV: Thank you.

(She tosses back her shot without wincing. He does the same. Neither eats.)

LYUBOV: I can help, but first, tell me, what sort of bride is it you want, Nikolai Nikolayich?

STYCHKIN: *Want*? The bride fate sends me.

LYUBOV: Then what do you need me for?

STYCHKIN: Well. . .

LYUBOV: You see, everyone has his own taste. One man likes brunettes, another likes blondes.

STYCHKIN: Well, I'm a down-to-earth man. . .

LYUBOV: You said that.

STYCHKIN: . . .a man of *distinction*.

LYUBOV: I know, I know.

STYCHKIN: And beauty, for me, at least *external* beauty, is secondary. For beauty is only skin-deep.

LYUBOV: That's what they say.

STYCHKIN (*pours out two more shots*)**:** I mean a pretty wife causes nothing but anxiety. I look at it this way: What matters most in a woman is not what is on the outside, but rather what lies *within*. I look into her *soul!* Eat something.

LYUBOV: Thank you.

(They clink glasses and throw back their shots. No one eats.)

STYCHKIN: Now. I would find it most agreeable if my wife were rather plump. But what really matters? The *mind*. And, truth be told, a woman doesn't need a mind, for she might think too highly of herself. Of course, we all must be educated nowadays, but there are many kinds of education. For instance, it would please me a great deal if my wife knew French and German. To be *multi-lingual*, now *that* would be very pleasing indeed. But what good is all that if the woman can't sew a button on my trousers, eh? I ask you. Myself, I am a man of the "educated class." I am just as comfortable with the Tsar as I am with you here now. But my ways are simple, and I need a simple girl. Above all, she respects me and feels that I have provided her happiness in life.

LYUBOV: Duly noted.

STYCHKIN: Now don't misunderstand. I'm not out to catch "the wealthy bride." No. Not at all. I have no desire to be a prisoner to a rich wife, a "kept man" if you will. I am a man of means. *However,* I simply cannot afford to marry a poor girl merely for love.

LYUBOV: Maybe we'll find one with a dowry.

STYCHKIN (*pours two more shots*)**:** Eat something, please.

LYUBOV: Thank you.

(They down their shots. No one eats.)

LYUBOV: Well then, my dear fellow. Have I got some bargains for you, some wonderful merchandise.

LYUBOV *(cont'd)***:** One is a French girl, another is Greek. Well worth the price.

(STYCHKIN thinks.)

STYCHKIN: No. No, thank you. Allow me, if you will, to ask now how much you charge for your services?

LYUBOV: Me? Not much. Twenty-five rubles, plus extra for the dress, which is customary, thank you very much. But then you have to figure in the girl's dowry. . . well, that's a different matter.

STYCHKIN: So *that's* where you clean up, is it?

LYUBOV: No no *no.* In the old days, when more people got married and settled down, prices were cheaper, it's true. But today what do we earn? I tell you if I make fifty rubles a month I fall to my knees and thank the Lord. I barely make any money on weddings.

STYCHKIN: Fifty?

LYUBOV: A *month!*

(Pause.)

STYCHKIN: So you think fifty a month isn't much?

LYUBOV: Of course not! Back in the old days we sometimes earned over a hundred.

STYCHKIN: I didn't think you could earn that kind of money in your line of work.

(He pours out two more shots.)

STYCHKIN: Eat, I beg you.

(They drink. No one eats. STYCHKIN looks her up and down.)

STYCHKIN: Fifty rubles. . .so then that would add up to six hundred a year. Eat something, I beg you. . .You know, Lyubov Grigoryevna, with those dividends you could easily make a match for yourself.

(She laughs.)

LYUBOV: Me?! I'm an old woman!

STYCHKIN: Not in the least.

LYUBOV: Oh, please.

STYCHKIN: No. Truly. You have a fine figure. And your face, it's so . . .plump and fair. . .

(They look at each other. Pause. STYCHKIN sits next to her.)

STYCHKIN: I mean . . . you are very attractive. If you found a man of means, who had a steady, practical job, and a little money in the bank . . . .why, with his salary and with what you earn . . . oh, he couldn't resist. I'm sure you'd live in perfect harmony. . .

LYUBOV: God knows what you're saying Nikolai Nikolayich.

STYCHKIN: What? I didn't mean anything. . .

(Silence. STYCHKIN blows his nose.)

LYUBOV: What do you make, Nikolai Nikolayich?

STYCHKIN: I? Seventy-five rubles, plus tips. . .Also, I make a little extra off of hares.

LYUBOV: So you're a hunter?

STYCHKIN: No. We call stowaways "hares."

LYUBOV: Oh.

(Silence.)

STYCHKIN *(getting up)***:** You know, I really don't need a young wife. I mean, after all, I am a middle-aged man, and I want someone who, who. . .well, someone who might be like you. You know, stable and mature. . .with a figure like yours. . .

LYUBOV *(giggles)***:** And God knows what you're saying.

STYCHKIN: What's there to think about?

STYCHKIN *(cont'd)*: You're a woman after my own heart. I'm a down-to-earth, sober man, and if you like me, well. . . what could be better?

(They laugh. Pause.)

STYCHKIN: Will you, will you. . . marry me?

(After a moment, they clink glasses. LYUBOV GRIGORIEVNA sheds a tear.)

STYCHKIN: And now, my dear, let me explain how life works. Look at me. Here I am, a strict and respectable man, a true gentleman. And I want my wife to be the same. I would hope that for her I would be her sole benefactor and, above all, the foremost person in the world. It's respect I need, *that's* the main thing, you know, respect.

(Lights out.)

END OF PLAY